# WRITINGS ON DANCE, 1938-68

# Writings on Dance
## *1938-68*

by

### A. V. COTON

Selected and edited by Kathrine Sorley Walker and Lilian Haddakin

Foreword by MARTIN COOPER

DANCE BOOKS

9 CECIL COURT, LONDON WC2N 4EZ

1975

I.S.B.N. 0 903102 20 X

# Foreword

## By MARTIN COOPER

Much the greater part of any daily critic's work is quite literally ephemeral. Born at night, often in discomfort and always in haste, it has a lifespan of hardly more than, say, twenty hours, after which it becomes at best a footnote to history and far more commonly so much waste paper. Even the wits and the penetrating observers among critics are defeated by the conditions of daily journalism unless their writing has not only a personal quality but, declared or undeclared, a theme on which each individual notice is a set of variations. A. V. Coton's writing about the dance had just that; and this was literally all I knew when I put his name forward to the Editor of *The Daily Telegraph*—this and the fact that I knew at once that I could work with him.

The nature of that underlying theme only gradually became clearer to me as I read his notices and listened to him talk about his work; but I confess that it is only now, after reading this anthology of his writing, that I have come fully to appreciate the profound seriousness of his approach to dance and the nature of his unrelenting opposition to those forces which, consciously or unconsciously, lower the status of the art, either by over-stressing the role of the individual dancer or by glamour-slanted publicity. That was in fact the underlying theme of all his writing: the importance of dance as a major art-form, perhaps the earliest and certainly one of the most demanding forms of self-expression—even, as he boldly puts it, one of the finest disciplines of 'auto-analysis' in existence.

Such a claim reveals the nature of the ideal that he had for the individual dancer, and it also explains the enthusiasm and understanding with which he wrote about dance-theatre and the many movements outside the main European, court-based ballet. He never in fact called himself a ballet critic, always a dance critic; and this insistence on the wider, less formal, and less enclosed world of dance reflected the nature of his character and his career. He came to the world of dancing through the theatre, but he already brought to the theatre the kind of experience that is very rarely

v

found among critics. Spells of service as a young man in the Merchant Navy and the Metropolitan Police Force had given him a knowledge of human diversity and an understanding of audiences, or at least potential audiences, very unlike the balletomanes of the London West End. His mental and physical horizons had been enlarged and he was freed in advance from the professional deformation of the typical critic, whose essentially indoor, urban world is too often bounded by the walls of libraries or theatres, and inhabited too exclusively by men and women of similar background and tastes to his own.

His work took him into a world where fashion and personalities counted large, but he thought little of fashion and judged personalities by the contribution they made to the art which they served. His preoccupations as a critic were before all else with dramatic truth and with humanity, with professional skill and professional objectivity of vision. No enterprise was too humble for him to give it his whole attention and the benefit of his own past experience, often in similar circumstances; and certainly no company was so exalted that it could escape his cool scrutiny. He was amenable to reason, but not—as many passages in this book show—to any other means of persuasion.

Although he called his early book *A Prejudice for Ballet,* any actual prejudice he showed within that world was for dance as an art of total human commitment rather than one of formal decoration, however exquisite. The zest of his writing about Antony Tudor and the Ballets Jooss shows this unmistakeably; but it is countered by the lyrical excitement of his detailed account of *Les Patineurs,* revealing the strength and the immediacy of his purely aesthetic reactions. To read such passages as these is to meet again the man he was, and no writer can ask for a better 'notice' of his life's performance.

# Biographical Note

A. V. Coton (Edward Haddakin) was born at York on 16 February, 1906; son of a railwayman; of mixed Irish and English extraction. He was educated at St Michael's College, Leeds. From 1922 to 1924 he was a merchant seaman, and he served in the Metropolitan Police Force from 1925 to 1937, mainly in Bethnal Green. He began writing ballet criticism in 1935 and became a full-time freelance writer in March 1937. He published his first book, *A Prejudice for Ballet* (Methuen), in 1938; in the same year he married Lilian Turner. He was also active in the organising and management of Antony Tudor's London Ballet, which was launched in 1938; and he worked with Peggy van Praagh and Maude Lloyd when the company was revived in 1939-40. From 1940 to 1945 he served in Civil Defence (Light Rescue Division) in the City of Westminster. (Light Rescue workers went into action during air raids, rescuing as many still-living persons as they could.) After the war he returned to freelance writing, diversified by lecturing (mainly evening courses in the London area) and by radio and television work; he was a founder-member of the London freelance branch of the National Union of Journalists. He published *The New Ballet: Kurt Jooss and His Work* (Dennis Dobson) in 1946. From 1943 to 1956 he was London correspondent of the American *Dance News*. He was best known in journalism as dance critic of *The Daily Telegraph*, a position he held from 1954 to 1969; but he also acted as assistant drama critic for the same newspaper from 1957, and throughout his career he was deeply interested in drama and the theatre generally. He was part author of *Ballet Here and Now*, published by Dennis Dobson in 1961, and, in the same year, President of the Critics' Circle, London. He travelled extensively in Europe and North America for the purpose of seeing ballet and other forms of dance, in performance and in teaching; he visited the U.S.S.R. in 1960. He died of cancer on 7 July, 1969.

# Editorial Preface

The aim of this book is to give some indication of A. V. Coton's conception of his role as a dance critic and of the range of his activity, in time, place and interest.

No writer on dance has set himself a wider brief. The writings from which this anthology has been selected extend over thirty years, in which he contrived to see nearly everything worth seeing in Europe and America in the sphere of theatrical dance. He wrote about it in three different styles which conditioned the presentation of his views: the daily press, with its limitations of space and tyrannical deadline; the periodical press, which allows of more detailed analysis, more developed themes, and frequently the chance of proof-corrections; and in books, the most satisfying medium of all. In each style, however, his guiding principles and criteria remained firmly established.

Three men dominate the text: Fokine, whose 'five principles' Coton wholeheartedly approved of as a measuring stick; and Antony Tudor and Kurt Jooss, each of whom, in the 1930s, provided him with personal revelations as to the scope and power of, respectively, Classical Ballet and Modern Dance. Because of the importance of this trio of choreographic creators to Coton's thought and reactions, they are represented at length.

Coton's concern with the native scene in Britain was always close, and his analyses of the historical development of English ballet, and of its strength and weakness, remain full of stimulating, and occasionally controversial, convictions.

He travelled widely, with regular viewing tours in Scandinavia, Russia, Germany, France, the Netherlands and the U.S.A., where so many lively developments were taking place, and he saw foreign companies as visitors to London. What he had to say about them makes illuminating reading, especially when he sums up the essence of some balletic legend, such as Galina Ulanova, in a few felicitous phrases. In this section on foreign ballet, so that the longer articles in which the background of a company is discussed can be balanced with the immediacy of a critic's first view of actual performance, the editors have combined, and at times re-ordered, a number of short notices into a more substantial piece of writing. Had Coton himself been engaged on compiling the book, he would no doubt have rewritten some of the existing material; without him, the only possibility is to re-shape. In the book as a whole, while we have made no alterations in matters of substance, we have sometimes slightly abridged our material for the sake of greater clarity and sequaciousness.

The critic's function was constantly in the forefront of Coton's mind. He cared passionately (as he did for every human issue) about the ethics of the job, about integrity in critic-artist relationships, and about the nature of the critic's contribution towards the well-being of his chosen art and its more just appreciation. No anthology of his writings could exclude his discussion of these matters.

What this short book cannot do is to reflect completely the comprehensiveness of his work. The entire scene of theatrical dance was of vital importance to him, which meant that he delved into its finances and management, into the realm of its preservation by film and notation, into matters of museums and archives and into the structure and state of training organisations everywhere.

Typically, he inaugurated in *The Daily Telegraph* a policy of what may be called 'whole-picture-representation' for the dance. Through this, the annual show by the larger dance schools, the main events of teaching congresses, the performing ballet clubs, the shoestring premiere by two dancers and a seventeen-year-old novice choreographer in any remote area of Greater London, and the budding talents in any regional centre, were assured of coverage as much as the first-ever performance of the Bolshoi Ballet at Covent Garden. Behind that programme, which was greatly valued by his wide readership, lay a network of carefully maintained personal contacts. Everyone active in the cause of dance, whatever the type or size of their commitment, knew they could approach him and be certain of his positive interest and forthright reaction.

# Acknowledgments

For permission to reprint previously published material we are grateful to the following: Associated Book Publishers Ltd. (for extracts from *A Prejudice for Ballet*, published by Methuen); Dennis Dobson (for extracts from *Ballet Here and Now*, edited by Susan Lester); Adam and Charles Black (for material from an essay on Beryl Grey in *Dancers and Critics*, edited by Cyril Swinson, and for the preface to Jane Winearls' *Modern Dance: The Jooss-Leeder Method*); the Editors of *The Daily Telegraph*, *The Dancing Times* and *The Spectator*; Mr Richard Buckle (*Ballet* and *Ballet and Opera*); Mrs Estelle Herf (*Ballet Today*); Mr Peter Williams (*Dance and Dancers*); we also thank Mr A. F. Leighton Thomas for permission to reprint, in shortened form, an article which appeared in *The Music Review* under the editorship of the late Geoffrey Sharp.

We owe special gratitude to Mrs Janet R. Davis for her unfailing encouragement, advice and help of many kinds throughout the preparation of this anthology. We are also much indebted to Mrs Myfanwy Shrapnel for her cover design; and for their very practical and valuable help—of various kinds and at various times—to Mr Harold Atkins, Miss Mary Clarke, Mr Martin Cooper and Miss Ludmila Mlada (Ludi Horenstein).

The frontispiece photograph is by Tania Stanham

# Contents

My concern with ballet today not only involves last night's performance, and the one I shall see tonight; it also embraces the sort of performances I am going to see in the future; and this is, for me, an inescapable attitude. It is also an inevitable one, having developed out of watching, with increasing interest, every performance I could attend in London since the mid-twenties.

If this is a lively art then it must be progressing, changing its forms and its ideas (however slowly) and the point of view with which the critic started in early days is no longer valid. His sympathies with the art, the artist and the artist's problems have widened and deepened. The more he sees the more he learns; and although some of what he learns will kill off one or two minor illusions, his increasing sympathy will embrace with understanding all sorts of problems of which at first he knew little or nothing.

... All critics keep on learning that in estimating artistic achievement and progress one can never arrive at a final viewpoint. Any night in any performance one may see a fresh miracle.

A. V. COTON
*Ballet Here and Now* (1961)

# I

# The Critic's Function

# The Critic's Function

Every dance critic—and A. V. Coton preferred to be called a dance rather than a ballet critic, as indicating a wider field of application—has individual views on his function and the ethics of his profession. The earliest of the declarations representing Coton's critical standpoint was in *A Prejudice for Ballet*, published by Methuen in 1938, and this is prefaced here by some comments on the book which he wrote in an article called "Revaluation" for *Ballet Today* in April, 1952, which in themselves present a valuable statement of a critic's equipment. They also, of course, refer to the other extracts from *A Prejudice for Ballet* which feature in the present anthology.

## ON *A PREJUDICE FOR BALLET*

In considering *A Prejudice for Ballet*, I should have liked to have had a wider experience of some activities in the world of dancing, to have looked for longer upon certain scenes but, all-in-all, I would write substantially the same book today if I were making a first attempt to get into written form my feeling, thoughts and general attitude towards the art of theatre dance. It is still a prejudice for ballet!

In 1937 I had been attending and studying ballet, and other kinds of theatre dance, for about twelve years and for a couple of years or so had been writing short notices and essays irregularly. This was the period before books-about-ballet were written in such quantities as they are now; there seemed to be a chance that a book with a fresh viewpoint might find a publisher. Most dance books in the British Museum contained some material which helped me to acquire a perspective on what was happening in (and to) ballet. Recollections of the quality of the new ballets created by the Diaghilev company during its final years plus the values suggested— but not realised—in the organisation of big scale ballet at that time, helped to establish a scale of values.

What then seemed the most important point was to look at, enjoy, and analyse *the whole work of ballet*—not just the performance of the individual dancers. It followed that the function of criticism could only be based on

3

a wide appreciation of all that went to make up the art of ballet—choreography, music, décor, production, as well as dancing. Remembrance of the
Diaghilev seasons of 1926/7/8 and 9; sympathetic interest in the work then
being done at both the Mercury and Sadler's Wells Theatres; attendance
at every sort of dance attraction on view in a London theatre—all this
helped to supply a background both of experience and research.

The book's main features were: analyses of the background and history
of ballet which supported my contention that "ballerina worship" wasn't
ballet-criticism; discussions on the functions of choreographers, composers
and designers; several chapters on the most important works of Fokine and
Massine; a special study of Massine's symphonic ballets; a detailed
examination of all the new works seen in one year, and finally, a reconstruction of the career and works of Massine up-to-date. It seemed then
that his novel ideas of ballet structure were the most vigorous and the
newest ideas that had come to ballet since the end of the Diaghilev régime.

I wrote with difficulty; much of the work was built in a stiff, heavy style
laden with sentences filled with subsidiary clauses; the book was, I think
only on occasion, didactic and solemn; more often it was outraged, bitter,
or vituperative. Its best feature (my unshaken opinion) was its analysis of
nearly every major ballet discussed in it. Where, at this distance in time,
do I think I was in error of judgment; where do I consider I said vigorously
something that needed saying?

Massine was credited with more inventiveness than, in fact, he continued
to show; I didn't guess the strength of the blossoming genius of Tudor;
also, I did not then see the historic value of the new dance-movement
being demonstrated by the Ballets Jooss. But I do not think I over-valued
the creative ability of the still-active Fokine and the fresh talent of Ashton.
The opinions on the unsuitability of music-critics as dance-critics, on the
danger to all critics who value the dancer above the ballet, on the proved
fact of quality declining in direct ratio to managements' playing down to
popular taste in an era of expansion—these I will stand by. I believe I am
as rational as a human may be and I am perfectly willing to be wrong—but
I've got to be proved wrong. I don't accept being told I am in the wrong by
someone I know to be more ignorant than myself; I demand argument,
evidence, persuasive logic. In contending that the essential basis for a
valuable system of criticism of ballet is "a prejudice for ballet", I am
convinced by the events of the past fourteen years that I was right!
Argue me out of that!

# THE CRITIC'S FUNCTION

*From A Prejudice for Ballet* (1938)

The critic is the most frequently misunderstood and unappreciated of all persons engaged in the production and elaboration of the complex processes constituting an art-form. The necessity of his function is continually being denied by everyone but himself. Actually the critic is recognised by the artist as the disseminator of information, the explorer into strange territory, and the obliging guide to all strangers coming into first contact with the form discussed; he is equally clearly recognised by the artist as the pedant who raps his knuckles for sudden and incomprehensible departures from the usual paths, who publicly upbraids him for the occasional and inevitable lapses into cheapness or triviality, and as the low fellow who is reserved and stinting of praise on those occasions whereon the artist surpasses all previous achievement. He is a great curse, a great necessity and a perpetual prick to the consciences of both the artist and his audience. The first-rate critic needs to be a writer of higher than journalistic standards, a man with a wide knowledge of the whole technique of the art-form discussed, and, wherever possible, something of a practitioner of the form. He must have a perpetually functioning determination to suppress all personalia and subjective preferences when engaged in assessing a particular work. The greatest critic is undoubtedly the man who has set out to create in an artistic medium, and early in the realisation of his poverty of executive and inventive ability has had the courage to refuse to continue as a third- or fourth-rate practitioner, and devotes his constructive faculty to the assessment and fostering of other men's works.

This almost superhuman list of requirements is rarely met with in one individual, but the better ranking of critical writers on the arts conform, in a major degree, to these standards. In spite of the fact that critical writing is hedged in with so many subjective considerations, there is a proportion at least as great as five per cent of writers on the arts who observe all technical progress, methods of teaching and publicising, and extensions of apparatus, with sympathy. Their observation, analysis, and encouragement produce the small corpus of objective criticism serving the great dual purposes of referring the work to its historic and sociological function, and of establishing its intrinsic worth in the living body of art.

When ballet began to develop as a complete and homogeneous art-form in Western Europe, gradually breaking away, very slowly but surely, from the Russian Imperial School tradition, it developed facets which called for a wider critical basis in its assessment. But the convention that ballet existed only as the handmaid of opera was deeply rooted, and ballet continued to be judged solely as a form of expression of music. No music critic had the faintest notion of what went on in the ballet school, how dancers were formed, or how a choreographer set to work, and the failure of at least half of all the Diaghilev ballets to get over the footlights what they had to put over is directly attributable to this particular perversion of criticism. Now the wheel has come full circle—with a vengeance—and the school of balletomane critics of ballet have seized upon the most obvious facet of all presentations of ballet, the dancer, and in place of the former little epics on the composer we now get an encyclopaedic series of monographs on the individual dancer. In the space of a very few short years this strange new art of ballet (concerning which, at first, few people were at all sure about its 'artness') has risen to the position of the most effectively publicised, financially secured, and completely misunderstood art-form in general circulation in the civilisation of Western Europe. As ballet was being driven through this hectic phase of development, the final factor essential to its success—specialist audience—had been developed by cinema, radio, and publicity. Cinema and radio had spread an awareness of the larger world without offering any effective remedy for the nostalgias aroused; but in London at least the post-1918 generation found in the crazy ballet of the experimental years the prime escapism from reality. The new spectacle offered a maximum of aesthetic satisfaction in its presentation of the materia of the motion picture, the picture gallery and the orchestral concert, fused in a technique of movement that referred to everything from the first Olympic Games to the most modern system of acrobatics.

The revival of grand ballet after the 1914-18 war heralded in a renaissance amongst the arts in Western Europe. Old standards everywhere were being dissected and analysed, resolved or rejected, and ballet, no less than any other form or combination of forms, was being assailed from without by the critical audience, from within by the choreographers: and Diaghilev, despite his personal preference for *ballet blanc* in its most exquisite manifestations, gave free rein for every form of experiment that his poets, musicians, painters, and choreographers wished to essay.

If there had been any percipient critics of ballet in that bright age—even though they might not all have been professors of dancing, or knowledgeable critics of other forms of theatre—they should have been very much struck by the easy and overwhelmingly uncritical acceptance of this complex and beautiful form, complete with all the temporary distortions that vogue demanded, by the generation which could find neither beauty nor direction in any other art manifestation. But a corpus of critical writing on ballet has been created on the over-simplified premise that the dancer is the only thing that matters. At a time when every standard of the former aesthetic was being mercilessly examined and experimented upon, ballet led the way as the prime vehicle of vogue in the theatre, and was drawing to it what no other art-form has ever had thrust upon it so easily, without condition of any sort, before—an absolutely ready-made audience, avid for the delights and thrills that only ballet could give, and totally devoid of any critical intelligence concerning the form. They accepted all too readily the critical premise that only the dancer counted—all the other factors were so many irrelevant additions to the bare bones of the dancing part. In ballet to-day, because too much emphasis had been placed on the dancer, and little or no criticism aimed at him, we are fast approaching the inevitable rot and decline which must ensue unless the general audience viewpoint concerning ballet and its worth alters; and that can only happen through a great revival of interest in and understanding of choreography, décor, and music, appreciated and respected for their intrinsic worth.

We have got a long way from the attitude (if it ever existed) that the choreographer is the most important person in the picture, first, last, and all the time in between. The artist in ballet does not exist who can function as the perfect choreographic artist should—devising the movement, writing the appropriate music, designing costume and setting, and re-hearsing the executants into their parts. Magnificent ballet has been produced by the collaboration of three diverse talents in the three essential media, a condition which has been accepted as the best possible arrange-ment since ballet began. The knowledge of these elementary facts alone should have been enough to awake perception and recognition of the necessity for a wide acquaintance with all the factors comprising ballet, on the part of every one in the audience. But a consideration of the greater part of the volume of written commentary reveals the existence of two conflicting, yet persistently upheld, premises: first, the dancer is everything in ballet, second, the music is all that matters. I can recall no critical writing on ballet which, dispassionately and with sustained emphasis, analyses and discusses every factor that goes to the making of ballet, and objectively assesses the importance and interdependence of every one of these factors. Sooner or later, the writer's personal inclination towards the major importance of either ballerina or composer is indicated, and the whole of the art-form is weighed and judged on the validity of only one of its component parts.

## FROM DANCERS AND CRITICS

Coton came back to the question of the critic and his work
twelve years later in an essay on Beryl Grey included in the
symposium *Dancers and Critics* edited by Cyril Swinson for
A. & C. Black in 1950.

A work of art is more than the sum of its parts and a critic is more than
the sum of his prejudices; they are his most obvious badge-of-office and at
the same time his most difficult burden. His predilections and preferences
will always be used for and against him in any discussion about his
influence on the art-form he writes about. Being human, the critic is
imperfect and is fully aware that he must for ever pursue the unattainable
ideal of "total objectivity", for all his views and his writings are based on
prejudices arrived at through all that he has learned, undergone and
discovered while living.

No critic worth the name is such a fool as to deny his prejudices, nor
does he belittle those of other critics because they differ from his own.
But it is important that they be clearly defined, strongly held while they
remain valid, and publicly disavowed when they are outworn. To mean
anything they must, it seems to me, be of a large and comprehensive order,
that is, prejudices for *kinds* of art and for *quality* in those kinds; they must
be big enough to enclose whole categories of history, entire theories of
aesthetics, complete battalions of artists. Above all, there should be
prejudice in favour of sincerity, originality, and all artists who show
humility towards their art.

My first book was titled, after much thought, *A Prejudice for Ballet,* and
in it I set out a summary of my experience of ballet and of the values
derived from that experience; it was an exposition of my requirements in
the art and in criticism of the art. I accepted no existing formula of
criticism and reviewed every work of ballet that had come my way which
supported, in some degree, my prejudices. It had taken twelve years to
formulate my attitude to this strange and eternally fascinating art; during
that twelve years my leaning towards *the whole work of ballet,* rather than
the dancing, or music, or décor, or any personality connected with the
work, grew firmer. I still believe that an important art should be discussed
and analysed and evaluated with scrupulous care—that is why I have
continued to assess any new work on, first, its choreography, and only after
that, on its degree of success as regards music, décor, idea and dancing.
Without good choreography there can be no good standard of dancing.
Every singer and player who ever interpreted Mozart's music is, in the
light of history, a good deal less important to the world than Mozart was;

so all the dancers there ever were or are can mean nothing without the creative opportunities given to them *only* by choreographers.

It would be tedious to analyse the first season of ballet I ever saw in an attempt to guess (at this remote date) at what it was that impressed me most. I was fortunate indeed, for I had never read a book on ballet or a newspaper notice, never talked with a balletomane of any vintage, when I saw my first performance. My innocence perfectly matched my ignorance when, one summer evening of rare leisure, I entered His Majesty's Theatre —and plunged head first into ballet (Diaghilev-style); and was luckily able to see a further nine or ten performances before that season ended. The dancers included Karsavina and Lopokova (with Trefilova as guest artist for some later performances) as well as Nikitina, Doubrovska and Danilova: the men included Woizikovsky, Idzikovsky, Lifar, Balanchine and Vladimirov. The repertoire of twenty-two works was nicely balanced between all the choreographers who had made—or were ever to make— ballets for Diaghilev: Fokine, Massine, Nijinska and Balanchine (except Nijinsky's *Faune*, his only surviving work, which was not given that season). Although I was ignorant about everything concerning ballet I had been a theatregoer for many years; and during my first thirteen years of ballet-going I spent my other leisure time in acting, stage-managing or directing plays with an all-the-year-round amateur society. This descent into autobiography is essential to bring the critical equipment into perspective.

Now the preference for the whole work of ballet, far from limiting one's capacity to judge dancing, is, in fact, the best possible method of measuring the exact value of every piece of dancing in the work. One judges the whole ballet by calculating exactly how the choreography expresses its creator's intentions *apropos* that ballet, and through this analysis of the choreography one sees all the contributory parts (idea, music, décor, costume, staging, dancing) in correct perspective. No good ballet ever came on to a stage without certain of its parts being up to a given high standard of quality; though too often we get mediocre ballets (i.e. good choreographic ideas blurred by poor music, slovenly décor and repetitive dancing, or, fine ideas and décor with interesting music tied together in dull, imitative choreography).

# II

# *Looking Back and Around*

# Looking Back and Around

PART ONE: 1943 AND 1945
From *Dance Chronicle*, July, 1943.
*Dance Chronicle* was a privately circulated journal which Coton
edited and largely contributed to during the years of World War II.

Ballet, a rigorously disciplined, very stylised code of movement of the human form, exerted for the joy of the beholder, emerges as part of the cultural expansion of European life about the end of the fifteenth century. It could exist only by Court patronage; Court and Church were the only sources of patronage and it was not in the Church's interest to direct attention to a pageantry which might rival the visual and oral pageantry of the Mass. Protection and financial help were granted by various princelings and nobles throughout the period that Renaissance influence went on leavening the basic Catholic mental make-up of European man. This gave a sufficiently stable development period to raise the art, by the early seventeenth century, to the status of a completely new theatrical form. But a century more had to elapse before the complete growth of that new theatrical type, the professional lay dancer.

1789: the French Revolution: the second great religion in the history of Europe is born: the religion of Man, which rocks to its foundations the religion of Christ. And immediately on top of this comes the very rapid expansion of the Industrial Revolution, these two events giving a complete change of colour to all European thought inside the half-century 1780 to 1830. Two strong factors combined to exert a powerful lever in shaping ballet as a fully developed form at this period: the flowering of Romanticism, and the growth of the bourgeoisie. The ideas and ideals loosed by the French Revolution had to be emotionally expressible in a formula which could fit the largest possible number of men. This concept helps to explain the tendency towards the Heroic which is manifest in much of the art of the period; and, in ballet, the tendency is very marked in the works of Viganò. His choice of subjects, his amazingly uninhibited treatment of his material, and his technically advanced theories make his the great ballets of the post-Noverre period. Under the impulse of Viganò, ballet

13

had become, as it were almost overnight, the theatrical medium best equipped to present the general social ideas of the time in a concise, recognisable and aesthetically satisfactory form.

The Heroic tends, as it has almost always done, towards the Romantic— the exaggerated, the lush, the oversize—and at this period it meant the vision of Man as a creature somewhat finer than God's image. The swelling tide of Romantic ideas in art hit ballet just when ballet was fitly developed to use all those ideas. And because industrial conditions were just then beginning to produce a numerically large class of people who needed a cultural apparatus which would apparently mirror their lives and aspirations, and seem to give them a justification, ballet of the Romantic genre blotted out every other sort of theatre dancing in existence. On a very large scale, because it was happening throughout the European theatre in each country undergoing the benefits of industrial expansion, art became— for a time—the required sort of "mirror of Nature". What the artists had to offer, in all sincerity, was exactly what the public needed.

When the Romantic influence waned amongst painters, musicians, dramatists and poets, it still weighed heavily with the choreographers, and outworn formulas were kept in use long after they had ceased to provide a true basis for the cultural expression of the times. This fact is obvious in the work of Perrot, Mazilier, St Leon, Taglioni and other choreographers up to Petipa. The justification of the latter's career is the creative ingenuity applied to the invention of choreography (although within the limited formulas defined by a previous age); and this ingenuity is worked out with the help of the immensely advanced technical resources created in the Russian hothouse out of the analyses and dissections of Blasis. At this period, although Content is a constant factor, Form is still to a certain extent experimental; therefore the Neo-Romanticism of Petipa, and his torch-bearer Ivanov, is historically justified. We can still learn from them, but not as much as we might be able to learn from the works of Viganò if they were extant, according to the evidence about him in existence.

From *Dance Chronicle*, February, 1945.

Petipa composed ballets for approximately fifty years, and so exerted an enormous influence over the art as practised in Russia during that period. When we reflect upon the impact of Romanticism on ballet in the early 19th century, and observe how its delayed-action effect served only to emasculate the art more and more as the middle years of the century rolled by, we must be grateful that any choreographer of over-average gifts occurred to bring some degree of stability into the ballet theatre. The collapse of ballet into trashy meaninglessness seems to have been staved off only by the exercise of Petipa's talents. For there can be no doubt that he had talent of a high order, and, if the definition of genius as "an infinite capacity for taking pains" is valid, then he certainly had genius during one phase of his career.

He composed every sort of ballet imaginable at that time, though the Romantic hangover during his early ascendancy governed the plot-types considerably; and there was no sufficiently strong dissension, about ballet inside ballet, to make him take any revolutionary step. Strategically judged, he is an example of "the inevitability of gradualness" in the shaping of ballet's ideology. He ranged over a vast field for subject-matter, choosing generally to create pictures of adventurous life in former epochs and under differently constituted societies, and seems to have handled his plots with an assured competence. He created about sixty ballets of which few have survived, yet his importance lies in the fact that succeeding choreographers and dancers have been inordinately inspired by the purely *dance* quality innate in those works. His achievement, in terms of *created dance,* on the highest level, has set a standard to which the greatest choreographers since have constantly referred.

In lay-out most of his works follow the convention of his day, ending with a divertissement, and though his handling of stage masses was masterly his great contribution lay in the development of the purely executive element, through the solo dances.

The two outstanding works associated with his name are *Le Lac des Cygnes* and *The Sleeping Princess.* In the former it is not possible to decide precisely how much Petipa, and how much Ivanov (then his chief assistant), contributed to the whole effect of this masterpiece. But *The Sleeping Princess* has come to us more or less intact.

Doubtless much of the fascination of these dances—unequal architecturally but including some of the most skilfully worked essays in pure classical terminology—lies in their offering such a contrast to our contemporary style of classical-dance structure. They have value as a stimulus to all present-day dancing, a stimulus which grows partly from their acquired aura (recollections of famous dancer associations and the magnificence of the Diaghilev Ballet) and partly from the demands they make on even the highest category of executants. Technically and interpretatively they are almost beyond the capacity of present-day dancers, not because today's dancers lack technical finish and subtlety, but because the producing system which enabled the dancers to squeeze the ultimate finesse of gesture, the last iota of style, out of Petipa's dances in Russian productions no longer exists inside the main channel of ballet. That finesse-ing and the circumstances under which it was displayed are part of a system which is gone for ever. Contemporary practice has trained audiences to expect some affinity between décor, costume, music and choreography —an affinity which could not occur in Petipa's day because true collaboration between the choreographer and his associated creators simply did not exist. Probably for this reason Diaghilev's production of *The Sleeping Princess* in 1921 was artistically a more harmonious achievement than the original 1890 version. Then, the dancers were all of quality unsurpassable within the terms of the balletic idiom of their day, but there would be lacking that cohesion between settings, costumes, stagecraft, and production generally which was so obviously (from the best recorded impressions) the *clou* of Diaghilev's production thirty years after.

Ballet exists in terms of time and space and because its presentation is always coloured by these two factors in many subtle ways, it undergoes a process of change, decay and revivification at every performance from the first onward. That any dances from a Petipa work in 1890 are still in existence is proof that the process of re-creation rather than re-production has been the one way in which the quality of the original work could be maintained alive and glowing.

But after Petipa, artificialities of manner in mime, dancing, musical composition and decoration applied to ballet have reduced the form almost to the point of death. By the early 1900s ballet is an imitation of imitations when Fokine comes on the scene. Fokine had the luck to be born at a time when every other art form had cast off, more or less successfully, the weight of Romanticism. For the first time since Viganò's and Blasis' period it was possible to look at the world through the windows of the ballet academy and see it as a place full of marvels and horrors, beautiful and terrifying. It was a world whose foreground was not exclusively occupied by the image of man and therefore offered a larger palette of colours to work with than any choreographer had used for a hundred years past. He was conscious of living in his own age; that age in which men were beginning to escape from the nineteenth century pipe-dream of perpetual stability. His was an age in which man was discovering again the splendour and beauties of past cultures and previous civilisations, and with the rest of the forward-thinking artists he realised that *all* living, *all* knowledge, *all* imagination were to be drawn upon by any artist using any art-form.

The physical possibilities that the Russian academic methods had produced in dancers and the unlimited materials as regards situation, time, place, subject, which the choreographer could draw upon were thus united for the first time when Fokine composed a ballet independent of plot, and independent of ballet conventions. Since Viganò, he is the first notable example of a choreographer who is fully trained academically, and who is fully disciplined as a personality. He was able to take a detached view of the Romantic Ballet that had coloured every part of the theatre background in which he learned his craft.

It is this non-attachment to conventional Romantic symbols that enables him to score a ballet in what looks like a Romantic formula, yet in which there are no human beings—either life size or exaggerated—and because he has no need to consider the human reactions of his characters, he can concentrate all inventiveness on the expression of pure forms of Dancing. The whole of his training, teaching, research and revolt is expressed in *Les Sylphides,* which is the distillation of the pure essence of ballet for the first time in the history of ballet. A work which—like all great art—is more than the sum of its parts is a work which has always something new to give us, and this can happen only because the ideas and memories which it evokes are not limited to any one phase of man's life. For this reason *Les Sylphides* is identifiable as the first truly classic work of ballet created out of four centuries of continuous history.

## PART TWO: 1961 (FROM *BALLET HERE AND NOW*)

When Diaghilev and his associates offered their reformed kind of ballet to the Europe of fifty years ago, they felt no compulsion to advertise their product by slogans. In common with other pioneers they could believe that their reforms were valuable enough to affect the entire system within which they were working, but they probably did not realise for just how long their passionate application of the new principles would go on being effective. Yet, in fact, the present century's renaissance of ballet stems directly from their work.

It is likely that a rebirth of an art-form can only come about when two minimum conditions are present: there must be strong cultural pressures which compel the makers of the art to effect reforms; and these reforms must show (or at least, seem to show) the application of new principles of the art.

We are here concerned to examine the basis on which the ruler and 'cabinet' of the Diaghilev Ballet worked and to find whether their new formulas have, by today, become outworn through fifty years of use and misuse. Half a century's achievement can be dissected for evidence to show that the heirs and successors of Fokine's reformation have kept faith with their artistic responsibility—or have betrayed it.

Even before Fokine began working closely with Diaghilev he was dissatisfied with the ballet system in Russia; his concern was, however, less with the raw material of ballet than with the manner of its use.

All those forces in the nineteenth century, such as widespread educational advances, technological developments, expansions in science and industry, changing forms of political rule, improved communications, and so on, which influenced the shape of life for Europe's millions, also influenced the culture which those millions consumed. These new ideas had affected the majority of Europe's artists and showed their impact, however diluted, in their work. But ballet-making, even in Russia, where it seemed more stabilised than elsewhere, was a closed world.

The special conditions surrounding Russian society, even those governing its ballet-making system, were not likely to have given Fokine any very clear-cut notions about the spirit of his times, nor to have driven him to much hard thinking on the theme of the Artist and His Duty to Society.

But he was an intelligent, cultured Russian with a respect for the art of which he was both a servant and a master. The quality of ballet, the corruptions and nepotism working in the companies, the lack of any regard for principles to be derived from Beauchamps, Noverre, Viganò, Blasis, forced him into an attitude of aggressive defence of the art's purity. His contemplation of current methods led to his defining certain simple, logical rules for choreography. These rules, he believed, could provide a platform on which the ballet-maker could build sensibly and securely.

At first he expounded these ideas in his notes attached to his synopsis for a ballet project on *Daphnis and Chloë* (1904). They were ignored at the time, and only when he began making a series of successful works for Diaghilev's company was it obvious that his ideas contained in the famous five principles* were sensible—and they worked. They were not really new discoveries so much as fresh thinking about the principles implicit in the structure of ballet since the art had ingested the last previous 'reformation'—i.e. the Romantic rediscovery of feminine frailty and spirituality. Once it was clear that they would produce results—as in, for

---

*Fokine's five principles are enunciated in his letter to *The Times*, 6 July, 1914; the text of the letter is given in Cyril W. Beaumont's *Michel Fokine and his Ballets* (1945), pp. 144-47. The principles may be stated as follows:
1. In each case, instead of merely combining ready-made and established steps, a new form must be created, corresponding to the subject, the most expressive form possible for the representation of the period and the character of the nation represented.
2. Dancing and mime have no meaning in a ballet unless they serve as an expression of its dramatic action; they must not be used as mere *divertissement*.
3. Conventional gesture may be used only where it is required by the style of the ballet; in all other cases gestures of the hands should be replaced by mimetic movements of the whole body. The dancer should be expressive from head to foot.
4. The principle of expressiveness is to be extended from the individual to the group; the dancing of a group and the combined dancing of a crowd must form an expressive part of the artistic whole.
5. There must be an alliance between dancing, music and scenic design on terms of complete equality.

instance, *Les Sylphides, Petrouchka, Le Pavillon d'Armide,* and *Prince Igor* —they began to influence, both consciously and indirectly, everyone actively working for the Diaghilev venture. They helped to incite that change of spirit, sharpening of imagination, and freshening of responsibility essential as first conditions for an artistic rebirth.

Between 1909 and 1929 Diaghilev presented a few ballet revivals, and about sixty new works which included eighteen ballets of Fokine staged between 1909 and 1914. Later, working in other countries and with various companies, he created in all sixty ballets before his death. None of these, from my experience and inquiries, departs in any significant particular from the conditions implicit in the five principles.

The principles were not, of course, positively taught as a kind of choreography-made-easy method; they had a more subtle impact on the ballet-makers who followed or worked beside Fokine both in Diaghilev's time and later.

Diaghilev could—and at times, did—take extraordinarily arbitrary views about what he and his collaborators were doing with and for ballet; he often overrode decisions made 'in cabinet'. But at no time was there any retreat back to the ballet-making formula which the exiles had left behind in Petersburg.

If today we study the scenarios, listen to the music, look again at the designs for scenery and costumes and, not least, refresh ourselves with the best surviving critical writings on those events of the Diaghilev Era, we see the principles justified. Diaghilev accepted the fact that Fokine had pulled down much of the old rococo mansion of ballet and had laid strong foundations for a new temple to Terpsichore.

Our present concern is: have the valuable choreographers since Fokine's day been skilful in following, adapting or even extending the Fokine formula? Have some of them twisted or perverted it for good reasons of their own? Has anyone proved that better and more immediately valid principles are available? Are there new ballet-making methods which sensibly surpass Fokine's as clearly as his seemed to surpass those of Noverre? (Yet, on analysis, Fokine's are not much more than a bold re-appraisal, in twentieth-century terms, of the ideas that Noverre had advocated and partly realised mid-way through the eighteenth century.)

If the astonishing output of the choreographers other than Fokine working with Diaghilev surprises us by its variety of forms, its novelties of thematic, musical, decorative, dancing and stagecraft treatments, yet we can see that it was a straightforward use of the Fokine method. Diaghilev might, on occasion, give added bias to one factor among the unison-of-parts deriving from the principles—but, in essence, the principles were the basic framework for all choreography.

He may have bidden one of his eccentric collaborators to astonish him—but none of the ballets suggests that he would have tolerated an astonishment based on a reversal of the formula which had, so far, produced a catalogue of works of an absolute novelty unimaginable before 1909.

His occasional decisions to give extra prominence to some sensationally gifted dancer or smart designer or fashionable composer were always calculated to add to the total *novel* impact of the new work. This successful 'sensation-mongering' was forced on him by his agonising need to keep his company, whether performing or resting, in full public view.

The other equally pressing need was, always, for enough backing simply to keep things going. So he began to be accused of purveying novelty merely for novelty's sake. From the perspective of today we may perhaps be grateful that such 'novelties' included for instance, Nijinska's two successes, *Les Biches* and *Le Train bleu*, the earliest crystalline choreography of Balanchine (*La Pastorale, The Triumph of Neptune, La Chatte*) which led with a kind of sensational inevitability to his lyrical and dramatic masterpieces, *Apollon Musagète* and *The Prodigal Son*. Also of this period were half a dozen Massine ballets, including those which showed a way for dozens of later choreographers to exploit themes drawn from contemporary life, and to use a vivid kind of luminous, new stage-craft—these were, *Le Pas d'Acier* and *Ode*. There were in this period handfuls of *décors* by Derain and Picasso, Matisse and Laurencin; and music by Stravinsky, Auric, Milhaud, Fauré and Prokofiev plus the dancing of such as Lopokova, Danilova, Doubrovska, Idzikovsky, Woizikovsky and Lifar.

But certainly the standard of dancing in the late years of the 1920s was lower than in the Golden Period of 1909-14. In 1914 the company was a complement of talent from the Moscow, Petersburg and Warsaw schools; by the 1920s there came an influx of English and Russian *émigré* dancers. Yet that second decade of the company's existence must be assessed on the always-changing repertoire of new works by Balanchine, Nijinska and Massine; and even in 1929 new talents were coming to Diaghilev's notice. Had he lived, Ashton and Lifar might have blossomed earlier as choreographers, for the studios of Paris, London and New York were full of potentially exciting dance talent, much of which got its chances when de Basil launched out three years later.

After Diaghilev's death there seemed to be a fallow period in which nothing happened, but in fact the current of his twenty years' activities was still flowing along all those channels from which it could, later, pour out into other and different dance organisations. During the period 1929-32 the first strong seeds of English ballet (which had, in fact, been sown during the preceding five years) were beginning to put forth their first strange blossoms. The three surviving Diaghilev choreographers were far from idle, being occupied as guest visitors making or reproducing in recognised ballet-centres, or for commercial enterprises . . . exactly as Fokine was doing and had been doing since he settled in America after the Russian Revolution.

The setting-up of the de Basil Ballet Russe (this is its best, easily identifiable title: during fifteen years it ran through seven or eight different identities) in 1932 was—and we can only now, in retrospect, define this change—as important a development for ballet as had been the first Diaghilev visit to Paris. The importance was only partly an artistic one; now ballet was entering a period in which, for the first time in seventy years (and even yet only intermittently), it could be operated, managed and presented as a commercial proposition. Whatever one thinks of the odd talents of Colonel de Basil (not all of them constructive or in the best interests of his dancers, his ballets, or his choreographers), at least he planned and set up a big-scale ballet company, equipped with top-line choreographic artists, who were adequately paid and given reasonably good material and collaboration. If now we forgive the hysteria and vulgarity of most of the publicity (some of it confected by former devotees of Diaghilev who might have known better) which acclaimed de Basil as the legitimate artistic heir of Diaghilev, we must recall with gratitude the man's activities.

It is quite possible that some equally business-like, equally unscrupulous, equally reckless business manager might have set up a similar ballet project soon after Diaghilev's death. But de Basil put into the European and American market a well-organised company with a large repertoire, much of which consisted of ballets inherited in faint condition from the Diaghilev company plus new works devised approximately on the Diaghilevian formula.

Soon there were other companies in the field, a not unremarkable fact when we realise that, as de Basil had quickly shown that his ballet interest was a fully commercial one, so other would-be impresarios, ballerinas with purses, and ambitious choreographers, were able to find backing to start companies to take advantage of the remarkable boom that ballet was enjoying. Now, of course, nearly thirty years after, we can clearly see the inevitability of the process; Diaghilev spent twenty years catering for an informed, moneyed, highly cultured, *avant-garde* European following, in which period he made ballet so attractive that it drew the interest of people who, but for his brand of the goods, would never have paused to look at dancing once in a lifetime.

By the early 1930s the Diaghilev-trained public was hungering and thirsting for something—for anything—that seemed to approximate to the Diaghilev kind of dance theatricals: another, younger but equally keen, public was beginning to realise what it had missed by failing to see the Diaghilev ballet of the 1920s.

Too many imponderable (and often non-ascertainable) factors lie at the back of a particular rise of popularity for an art. At this point in ballet's history we can note only these facts (but they are *facts* of ballet history): (1) cultural, political and social pressures over most of Europe in the nineteenth century had led to a decay in ballet, both expressively and ideologically, (2) the changed social climate of the early twentieth century provided incentive and conditions for a revaluation of the aims and the idioms of ballet, (3) Diaghilev and his associates launched their reform movement and, for twenty years, advanced those fresh ideals and idioms in every worthwhile centre of the Western world. A basic change in what ballet was *for*, what it was *about*, how it did things in *new ways*, had been brought about. The climate of the times had displayed this fresh kind of theatricality to a public avid for a novel, truthful and powerful aesthetic experience. This was the kind of ballet which had long been out of vogue in Europe: one based essentially on atmosphere, suggestion, indirect comment on its subject-matter. A cultural cycle had been completed and Western audiences were ripe for a fantasy kind of theatre which made its impact not chiefly through story-telling, but by firing the imagination and stirring the senses with riotous colour, music and dancing.

Perhaps this somewhat simplifies the action and impact of ballet; within the art and the craft there are innumerable variations of form and style, hundreds of delicately different formulas for the balancing of the visual and aural appeals of music, spoken words, *décor* in paint and in light, disciplined mime, elaborately stylised movement and gesture. It is the knowledge and skill with which these subtle components are handled that define true choreographic craft, used to reveal and illuminate true choreographic imaginings—which are much rarer than a majority of ballet followers realise; and this leads directly again to consideration of the Fokine principles.

We must assess from the evidence of actual performances seen during the past thirty or forty years how far the Fokine principles were proved good by those who followed him as choreographers, working with organisations that we can reckon artistically valuable. It has many times been emphatically stated, by people with lifelong involvement in the business of dancing, of training dancers and of making ballets, that choreography cannot be taught. This view has arisen, completely honestly, simply because no great pedagogue of the dance art has set down in literary form an analysis of the *craft* of choreography. Had some latter-day Noverre or Blasis or Delsarte arisen, fifty, or fewer, years ago, such a treatise could very well have been in circulation and by now be making an impact as powerful as did, in their heyday, the documents on theatre principles that Noverre, Blasis and Delsarte wrote.

As with crafts of music, sculpture, painting, and architecture—to name only those most nearly parallel to dancing—the elements of choreographic structure are ascertainable and can be taught. It is by no means unlikely that teachers of the calibre of George Balanchine and Marie Rambert do, in fact, teach choreographic craft—but by unannounced, indirect means. Too many dancers, teachers, and would-be choreographers rely heavily on the *mystique* that choreography is something inborn (like having flat feet, cross eyes, albinism or other ills that human flesh is heir to). They create by trial-and-error, throwing away in the rehearsal room what dancer-models have achieved through kilograms of nervous expenditure and sweaty endeavour, when a little planning in advance on lines laid down like algebraic formulae could produce movement patterns at least as original as *tachiste* paintings by chimpanzees. There is a feeling almost of terror, among ballet's workers, that choreography should be thought of as a sensible craft—which, of course, it is; or nothing would have survived from the past (*vide* any literary comment on or by Noverre, Beauchamps, Arbeau, Viganò, Petipa, *passim*).

It is not that choreographers wish to maintain their trade as a closed guild; simply, they are defending themselves against any hint that the process of movement-creation involves the intellect. When they can talk about their work—fortunately not often and not many of them—they can utter more sententious rubbish about 'my art' than does the average twenty-year-old action painter or atonal composer. In fact, few of them have a clear notion how a choreographic concept will develop in its middle and later sections when they start work on the dancers. They rarely put down on paper, either in notation or long-hand, what they hope to produce, relying (nowadays, far too much) on picking up some movement suggestion out of what a dancer does unconsciously in the rehearsal room. A top-line choreographer will invariably have a complete design worked out in terms of space and time when he starts rehearsing; and will be ready to find (will, indeed, expect) that some oddity of movement by a dancer will make a starting point for a fresh, unimagined variation on the main theme, or a fresh melodic twist in the continuo of the movement pattern. But he will

not allow these accidentals to grow into the dominant style of the dance patterning.

The apprentice architect learns how to copy plans, how to look at a building so that he can reproduce its original plan, and how the various trades on which he relies for results are operated. He must know a certain minimum about bricks, stone, cement, steel, timber and metal-work. The young composer learns one or more instruments thoroughly, studies the style of music-making during several centuries, acquires knowledge of mathematics, acoustics and aural aesthetic; he studies the laborious business of notations and instrumentation, voice production and conducting, etc. In the same way a choreographic apprentice should study (not merely by watching and taking part in other peoples' ballets) the techniques of all commonly known dance styles—the main European folk modes, ballroom dances of two centuries, the social dancing which led to ballet. He should have a thorough classroom grounding in academic ballet, modern stage styles and ballroom dancing developments since 1900. He should know a minimum of geometry, to facilitate working out space patterns which look original, mathematics and music so that his visual and aural components can be blended suitably and needs, at least, an intelligent non-specialist's awareness of political and social history. His knowledge of lighting, stage-management and dramatic production should be as good as those of a director of, say, a provincial repertory theatre . . . and he should be able to forget completely the movements of every ballet in which he himself ever danced. This is the basic technical knowledge he requires as a springboard from which he can effectively launch his imaginings.

The evidence of the Diaghilev ballets and their performances and what has been recorded about the deliberations of Diaghilev and his 'cabinet of advisers' suggest that the business of treating choreography as a *mystique* was the rule then. It is observable that Fokine was a great choreographic innovator, and it is equally observable that there was no policy of guiding other choreographers to note his works and then go and do likewise. The conditions in which Nijinsky, Massine and all the others had been trained and inducted into ballet were those of the cast-iron disciplinary system of Russian Imperial Ballet, in which there is almost no evidence that choreography *as a craft* had ever been taught to anybody. Such analyses as have been published comparatively recently reveal that the major figures among nineteenth-century Russian choreographers and *régisseurs* laboriously worked out their own formulae for using dance-style, musical background and miming technique. And the professional atmosphere kept rivalry boiling all the time: no master choreographer but thought that what he had 'discovered' for himself was worth keeping to himself until the grave should claim him.

No part of this supposition is aimed at belittling the talents of the Diaghilev choreographers. With very few exceptions (far fewer than have been obvious in the output of later international ballet companies) their ballets were theatrically effective dance-creations using music, *décor*, stagecraft, mime and movement, of surprising strength and quality. Lacking enough detailed record from any Diaghilev choreographer about his working methods, we must assume that each worked undeviatingly and uncompromisingly to create ballets which should, at least, differ in style and kind from the ballets that had been their background and apprenticeship in Russia.

Amongst them, Massine and Balanchine have certainly shown ample evidence that they have studied, assimilated, and probably effected mutations upon, the choreographic notions implicit in the reliable dance literature of the past three centuries. And each underwent, but under differing conditions, that sort of tuition that Diaghilev personally gave: the discussions about music, the inspection of paintings and architecture, the visits to museums and opera houses. In individual ways each Diaghilev choreographer after Fokine contributed to his ballet-making such ideas as could be absorbed there and then from all the European arts, and not least the art of ballet as practised in that company, where the outstanding exemplars, monument-high, were the still extant dozen or so works created by Fokine before 1914.

The fact that the ballet world is in the main made up of companies of dancers living in an atmosphere of almost monastic retirement from ordinary affairs renders its inhabitants peculiarly susceptible to the impact of each other, as individuals and as performers. The basic repertoire of all companies of international standing holds a number of common ballets inherited from the nineteenth century and from the early Fokine period. This latter fact is a fortunate aberration solely due to the fact that no one in the heyday of twentieth-century ballet had the wit to protect choreography by copyright. All Fokine's ballets are wide open to use, abuse, misuse, misinterpretation or plagiarism by anyone knowing a former Fokine-ballet-dancer who remembers their choreography even semi-accurately.

Dancers 'live' dancing as no actor or singer ever lived his performing material; the daily classroom routine is the ABC of that vocabulary out of which all ballets are made. The fact of a ballet being created, largely, on the specific movement qualities of the dancers it uses gives it a certain sort of inevitable topicality; this is precisely the measure of its fragility, its ephemerality.

No surviving ballet ever looks exactly as it looked when first given; by its nature it cannot, and we have long accepted—even if reluctantly—that an 'old' ballet is not so much revived as recreated (reassembled would be better), and always in a different shape and style than before.

Everything conspires to make ballet a transitory art-form; true choreographic imagining of the highest kind is of the quality of Picasso's restless experimentation—a non-stop series of new assessments of what can be done afresh with the angles and curves and masses and balances of that splendid instrument, the human body.

There is always a sense of vast expenditures of imagination and sheer physical energy, to be realised in a work which may last twenty minutes and survive twenty performances; this sense of prodigious effort for minute results affects all who take part in making and dancing ballets. It is part of the price gladly paid for the achieving of a moment of fresh lyricism, a phase of real beauty in movement. We are aware of the heavy cost in effort, in imagining and in detailed presentation, to choreographer and dancers. Any idea will suggest that its nucleus can be forced into an expressive shape through movement allied to appropriate music and *décor*. Everything in the ballet system conspires to make the choreographer attempt to be new, different, if he is to make good. Yet every single factor around him must show him that whatever he wants to do has already been done—or so nearly done as to force him into *any* expedient to give his new concept an air of novelty.

This is part of the occupational risk of the choreographer. Other theatrical creators have the use of words—which can often hide the sterility or ineptitude of the ideas behind a play, sketch or opera. He works with bodies and they have but a limited range of movements, and a remarkable visual similarity occurs, except with the better sort of dancers, when those movements are made . . . Perhaps this is to see the choreographer's problems at their blackest; but certainly he can never quite realise his first, fair imaginings to the full—unless he can plan works wholly in terms of known dancers whose movement potential he *exactly understands* from previous collaboration.

With the majority of valuable choreographers since Fokine, his principles appear to have saturated their outlook and practice—but, probably, almost wholly subconsciously. Excepting the inherited 'classics' (and, in this country, a small number of full-length ballets, all of recent date) every ballet that he will have seen, or danced in, will conform to the norm established by Diaghilev. That is, a one-act depiction of character: an atmosphere: a closed dramatic situation: a movement-suite as rigid in form as a music-suite.

It may occupy anything from fifteen to fifty-five minutes; it may have one or many scenes; it can be performed by a soloist or a duo, and it might not seem overloaded with forty dancers; its visual aids of costume, setting, properties, lighting, furnishings, can touch the utmost limits of their craftsmen's invention . . . but it is a one-act statement in movement composed of a mingling of the five requirements fixed by Fokine. So, a performance needs to be built out of a number of works in differing *genres,* if a wide but balanced range of effects is to be projected to the audience.

Looking back on all the ballets achieved since Fokine created *Les Sylphides* one is persuaded that these—literally thousands—of short ballets have been possible only because their makers had had to accept, as a practical working basis, the notions embodied in his five principles. Nobody alive can have seen every existing ballet (a feat that would have been quite possible to a ballet-goer fifty years ago who possessed a deep pocket-book and a passion for travel). A consideration of trends in ballet-making today must be based on examination of the methods of the choreographers who are the legitimate heirs (whether they knew it or no) of Fokine. They have influenced (and affected) one another—mostly indirectly—and their product is an offshoot or derivation or honourable borrowing from the five choreographers who served the Diaghilev Ballet. Apart from the somewhat tortuous, and occasionally magnificent, achievements in Soviet Russia, all significant ballet creation in our century is their work.

The history of choreographic development since the Diaghilev era centres, at its most significant, on the activities of the choreographers who survived him, on those bred out of the English renaissance of ballet, and on the Russian-accented achievement among the ballet companies of the United States.

De Basil formed his company in 1932 and both Balanchine and Massine worked with him for a while; but soon Balanchine left for America where he has been uninterruptedly active since. Massine remained as principal choreographer with de Basil until a split arising from disputation about choreographic copyright led to the founding of another big-scale company, of which Massine assumed artistic control. Then, during the war years, in America, he worked for every company to be found there; since 1947, when he first revisited Europe, he has occupied himself in freelance activities.

Apart from Massine's ballets (and those inherited from the Diaghilev collapse) de Basil made regular use of only one choreographer, David Lichine*, whose achievement since, largely in America, has been in minor keys. In recent years he has worked on the Continent, and for the London Festival Ballet.

During the 'ballet war' of the middle 1930s, when Massine had left the de Basil company, another rival group was the one headed by René Blum, for which Fokine was persuaded to leave temporarily his American occupations. His splendid revivals of some early works (from the pre-1914 era) and the creation of four ballets new to London, proved to be his European swan-song.

It was at this time that Nijinska, also a survivor from the late Diaghilev period, was working in Paris and also staged some revivals and made a few novelties for the English Markova-Dolin Ballet.

The English ballet renaissance almost exactly coincides with the period of commercial expansion following Diaghilev's death in 1929. Its most significant achievement was the setting-up of an institution that proved capable of breeding choreographers on a scale much larger than the Diaghilev enterprise had done.

The singular quality of this institution—the Ballet Club at the Mercury Theatre—was the insistence of its director, Marie Rambert, on making mountains of choreographic achievement out of molehills of green raw material. In this smallest of Europe's professional theatres, all but one of the important choreographers who became the firm pillars on which our ballet of today is founded were trained, tested and encouraged.

The completely unforeseeable condition of this theatre laboratory was that the smallness of its stage—and the equally small quantity of dancing, decorative and musical resources available—would force the dance creators to invent, expand and manipulate in a hundred different ways a completely new style of ballet-making.

Elsewhere in Europe there had been small-scale groups making what can be called 'chamber-ballet', but there is no record of their being exclusively occupied in creating an entirely new kind of ballet—as were the artists working under Marie Rambert in the 1930s. The Mercury Theatre achievements provided overwhelming evidence—if such were needed—that the Fokine principles were the only practicable basis for choreographic experiment at this time.

*Lichine died in July, 1972.

A survey of all ballets made at the Mercury, and a close analysis of the styles of Ashton, Tudor, Howard, Gore and Staff would show that each of them was working in a method which, subconsciously at least, was a total and unquestioning acceptance of these principles. New ballets were in new forms of movement; all movement was used to serve dramatic or expressive ends; every dancer was an integral and integrated part of the desired action; music and *décor* were indissoluble parts of the whole process of choreography. They were made on, and for, this smallest of professional stages, and the original concept of each of them was conditioned by the need so to use dancers, music, *décor* and stagecraft that the fullest choreographic expressiveness was reached.

This consideration presented to each choreographer such problems as: the most effective way in which to utilise duration of dance-phases; impact of the music; dramatic tensions between the several characters; visual impact of each costume, property or piece of scenery, and so on, and they were problems of a kind and intensity never before affecting the choreographer so profoundly at his task. This was being done on a stage, and with resources, ludicrously minute when compared with all previous balletic achievement of a professional kind.

As the craft of the miniaturist differs from that of the easel painter, the jeweller's from the sculptor's, the sonneteer's from the epic poet's—so the kind and degree of craftsmanship required at the Mercury Theatre differed (and in ways that were not easily apparent at first) absolutely from the ballet-making methods possible and customary in a 'normal', opera-house-sized, context.

But what, later, proved incontestably the perfection of the Mercury Theatre system for intimate ballet-making was the fact that not only could the choreographers easily adjust themselves to working conditions in larger theatres, but many of the Mercury ballets themselves could, with only minute adjustments of their space-patterns, be transposed successfully on to stages five or even ten times the area of the Mercury Theatre stage.

Now, on no other occasion has the art of ballet been faced with such a challenge; nowhere else did the conditions seem at first so unpropitious as they were here in London during the early 1930s. There was little money, few dancers, and limited opportunities for either the making or the showing of ballets; yet the atmosphere of the times and the unusual qualities of the differing kinds of leadership supplied by Marie Rambert and Ninette de Valois led to the creation of a phenomenal list of works, many of them masterpieces. The de Valois mechanism proved to be an existing opera theatre, complete with orchestra, which was technically a smaller-scaled version of those Russian (and earlier, French, Italian and

German) theatres in which ballet had been developed during the previous two centuries. Ninette de Valois's task was one of her own choosing—to establish a repertory ballet system approximately modelled on the system of the traditional opera-and-ballet houses of Europe, but, ideologically, based on the better achievements (as she saw them) of the Diaghilev company with which she had worked for some years.

From the start of the period of regular programmes at both the Mercury and Sadler's Wells, it was obvious that two quite distinctive sorts of English ballet were emerging; the Mercury formula leading to the highly individual sorts of ballet which Ashton, Tudor and the other Mercurians created, while the Sadler's Wells system, organisation and policy encouraged a continuation of the Petipa method, as it seemed workable to a director who was once a member of the Diaghilev Ballet.

Choreographers work as much from example as do composers, sculptors, painters, dramatists: they are influenced, irritated and stimulated by watching, analysing and performing (sometimes) the common repertoire of their day. There are no such things as texts for ballets, which reveal their content in the same way as do play scripts, opera libretti or music scores. Systems of notation for dancing have been continuously devised almost since the day ballet emerged as a science of movement. Yet even the most comprehensive of them is difficult to learn and read, and can only be translated into a basis for a fresh stage production by a skilled choreographer-dancer.

The choreographic hard core on whose achievements the success of both Ballet Rambert and the Sadler's Wells Ballet was built up consisted at first of Frederick Ashton, Ninette de Valois, Antony Tudor, Andrée Howard. In the very earliest years, Susan Salaman made a few ballets at the Mercury, and after the mid-thirties both Walter Gore and Frank Staff were creating, as well as dancing, for this company. The four principal founding choreographers of English ballet made between them forty out of the forty-five new Mercury ballets between 1930 and 1937 (this was the year in which Tudor left Rambert); in the same period Ashton and de Valois made thirty-nine ballets for Sadler's Wells.

Because of the chronology of their births, dance-careers, work in different companies, each of them was inevitably conditioned by and towards the Fokine-type short ballet. No English ballets of the Victorian and Edwardian eras survived the 1914-18 war; Diaghilev had shown one full-length ballet here in 1921; a few smaller visiting companies had shown short versions of, or excerpts from, some full-length nineteenth-century ballets. Apart from these examples and stimulators, the only other available repertoires which all these choreographers might have seen and studied were those of Diaghilev and of the Pavlova Company. Apart from Ninette de Valois (who made only one ballet for Rambert), these choreographers moved through their apprenticeships guided and goaded by Marie Rambert, whose scale of production and balletic values had been built out of her experience, first with Dalcroze, and her fruitful years with Diaghilev. Quite simply, here and at that time, there was no other acceptable method of ballet-making than the formula of the Fokine one-acter. Nowhere else in the Western world, where there might conceivably be chances of working on a bigger scale than at the Mercury, was there enough money, personnel and lively dance-creative talent.

What matters most in discussing choreographic styles and the use of ballet's raw material, is to note how these creators were developing the whole balletic craft by using themes, stories, atmospheres, in ways wholly different from those that served their great mentors of the Diaghilev company. Ashton soon showed himself a capable exponent of the romantic story-ballet and made further excursions into a field of 'pictorial' ballets based, usually, on suites of music, i.e. *Leda and the Swan, Mars and Venus, Florentine Picture, Les Masques, Capriol Suite, The Tartans* and *Façade.* Later he made ballets in modes derived from Fokine, Massine and Balanchine—but always showing individual choreographic imagining and invention.

In recent years his talent has shown itself at its highest in passages of marvellous dance-invention—particularly for the ballerina and most notably for Margot Fonteyn—such as *Symphonic Variations, Tiresias, Scènes de Ballet, Rinaldo and Armida.*

His other bent of invention has been the reconstruction from earlier scores and scenarios of new versions of *Sylvia, Daphnis and Chloë, Cinderella, Romeo and Juliet* (in Copenhagen), *La Fille mal gardée, Les Deux Pigeons.* His *Ondine* (1958) used an old scenario afresh and a new score in creating a pure triumph for Fonteyn. Ninette de Valois worked on the dramatic and narrative ballet with a complex story (often not clarified either by scenario or action), of which some of the better examples are: *Les Douanes, The Wise and Foolish Virgins, The Haunted Ballroom, The Rake's Progress, The Gods Go a-Begging, Checkmate* and, since the war, only *Don Quixote.*

Andrée Howard* has made fewer ballets than any of her contemporaries, circumstances having conspired to create no role for her inside the administrative or artistic staff of any company for any length of time; consequently hers have always been freelance activities, and the conditions

*Andrée Howard died in April, 1968.

in English ballet have worked to the disadvantage of the freelance. Her movement invention is less remarkable than that of the other of our ballet founders, but hers is a wonderfully feminine approach to both story and characterisation not equalled by that of any other living classical ballet worker (I am thinking, primarily, of Martha Graham as the exception). Though Miss Howard has a firm mastery of dance styles and can compose usually with nice fluency for either male or female dancers, her great quality is to invest her choreography for females with an exquisite and luminous femininity. Each of her characters is a precise and individual person bearing a clearly original choreographic signature. In a later assessment of English twentieth-century ballet, Miss Howard may be accounted one of the few choreographers of her time who could make her female characters earthily believable and yet could always invest them with dignity, grace, and splendour of personality. She is one of the very few living choreographers who never choreographically denigrates either sex for the sake of glamourising or canonising the other.

Antony Tudor, all prejudice apart, has to be reckoned one of the four most important choreographers living in the twentieth century. He started studying with Rambert in his late teens, danced, taught, played the piano, kept the accounts, stage-managed, created ballets, until he broke away from both the Mercury and Sadler's Wells (he was active simultaneously in both places for a while) in 1937 to form his own company. He was engaged as one of the creators of the new Ballet Theatre in New York in 1939 and, except for a few visits to Europe as guest choreographer, he has remained in America, making a few ballets and mostly now devoting his time to teaching.

From the very start, his was a unique talent, fostered, bruised and whipped on by Rambert's shrewdness and passionate interest. His early ballets, on subjects similar to those used by Ashton and de Valois, had a distinctive difference of style. The movements were more economical and (as in the work of few choreographers ever) they both merged with, and seemed to grow spontaneously out of, the music. He displayed an astonishing depth of knowledge of human behaviour and its many kinds of motivation; he could invest characters with precise and instantly observable frailty, charm, acerbity, dignity, folly, tenderness, wisdom, heroism or baseness. He had an incomparable gift for choosing the unexpected notion for a ballet, so that his scenarios have an individual oddity which sets them in a category apart from those of others. His interest in the reasons for, and the impulses of, action led him to concentrate on details of action, gesture and posture (quite apart from conventional dance steps) which should reveal normally unnoticed facets in a dance-personality. He would rehearse for five hours to obtain and fix in unique movement five seconds' worth of perfect illumination of some character's activity. He has been called "the first psychological choreo-grapher"— a cumbersome honour to wear. Better, his ballets can now be seen as the first continuous attempt, in this century's ballet-making, to show through dance and action the reasons for his characters' sufferings, elations, despairs, magnificences and—where textually valid—their abysmal meanness, vulgarity or selfishness.

Later in the 1930s both Walter Gore and Frank Staff, Ballet Rambert dancers, began making ballets: Gore with a leaning towards the expression of intense passions between the sexes and also to the amusing or astonishing exploitation of grotesqueries of character. Staff used a simple and rarified lyrical movement style for his serious subjects, developed a unique type of surrealist choreography for amusing or ironic scenarios, and was equally effective with ballets on human follies and foibles which he could illuminate with disrespectful burlesques. With Andrée Howard he shares the noble virtue of choreographically treating the sexes with equal seriousness, tenderness and respect.

This account may so far have seemed to emphasise heavily the activities of the Diaghilev group of choreographers and their English counterparts. But, in fact, elsewhere in the Western world (for Russian ballet, turned into Soviet ballet, went its own curious way, maintained a special strength, but made no artistic contact outside) there was little valuable activity any-where. In Italy, the art had sunk back again to the level of being mere opera-decoration (this in the country which had fostered the original notions from which the entire science of ballet has developed!). France had perfected a teaching and performing system within a series of State Theatres (mainly Parisian); but in no other centre is there so variegated an audience, such fluctuations of both taste and fashion, such an insub-stantial public. A joyful cynicism is part of the French dancer's professional equipment and nowhere else does dance skill count so lightly alongside charm and adaptability of manner. Only in Russia do politics play as clear a part in balletic organisation as they do in France.

Denmark had its own brand of antique classicism, the Bournonville repertoire carefully maintained in Copenhagen. But in Sweden, Finland, Austria, Switzerland and, indeed, most other countries there was the same artistic sterility which had begun to creep over the ballet systems of Russia and France. Holland and Finland had no native ballet system and no national opera before the inter-war period of the 1920s and 1930s. Wherever, in the small European countries, there was an attempt at introducing or resurrecting ballet, it came *after* Diaghilev's company or some smaller Russian troupe had shown the effects of the Fokine formulas.

During these inter-war years some groups developed a special character as frameworks for a few ballets of quality—these being the companies retaining the services of choreographers of some degree of competence and invention. Where these companies had something worthwhile to show, the ballets had been made by pioneers directly guided and trained by older choreographers and teachers who had left Russia to settle in the West.

Bolm and Mordkin can be claimed as direct inciters of the first lively American ballet activity this century; both had settled there (Bolm,1917: Mordkin, 1923) and opened schools, ran performing groups and helped young Americans to fight their way into the higher ranks of dancing and choreography. Fokine, too, had left Russia soon after the revolution of 1917. By 1923 he was settled in America, teaching and producing. When Balanchine went there in 1933, his arrival coincided with the first visit— and the shattering impact, too—of the de Basil Ballet Russe on its first visit; a catalytic event which brought into lively activity almost all the ballet potential in the country. But it should be remembered that before this explosive event made its impact, three local companies (in San Francisco, Philadelphia and Chicago) had been successfully active in continuously staging new ballets on dancers produced from schools mostly run by Russian émigrés. Their choreographers had all trained at some time with ex-choreographers or ex-dancers of the Diaghilev group, either in Europe or America.

Sweden had been visited by Fokine in 1913 and 1918, when he staged some of his early period ballets in Stockholm (certainly until very recently his own production of *Les Sylphides* was still in repertoire, with a clarity and aesthetic precision that I have seen matched only in his final London production of this work in 1936). From 1931 until his death in 1955 Julian Algo, part-Spanish, part-German, was in charge at Stockholm; he encouraged both ballet and modern dance choreographers and his type of *ballet d'action* reflected ideas derived from both Massine and Laban . . . and a somewhat similar state of affairs was to be noted in every other corner of Europe which had undergone its own local ballet revival at some time after 1910.

In Germany this had been a delayed-action process; from the mid-twenties, until Hitler decided that all art was decadent, Laban and Wigman and a large flock of their followers and pupils worked with the new kind of dramatic dance that persists under the inept title of 'Modern Dance'. Both Laban and his chief disciple, Kurt Jooss, were compelled to leave Germany in 1933, but both found refuge and opportunities to continue their work in Great Britain. The Hitler era in Germany was one of little theatrical activity of value; and similarly there was no free experimentation or artistic vitality in the Italian Theatre of Mussolini's time.

After the war, when the arts could begin to function again openly in Western Germany, ballet had a minor re-birth. Its fantasy-and-escapism elements made a strong appeal to the well-starved imaginations of the war's survivors. Such small amounts of pure 'Modern Dance' as had, in the Hitler era, been permitted to infiltrate the German theatre were now almost totally superseded by ballet.

But this was not a 'straight' kind of ballet, either classical or neo-classical such as the English, Americans and Scandinavians had brought forth in the past quarter-century. It was a kind of 'opera-house ballet' which—inevitably, I think—could be the only kind with an instant appeal in a country whose theatres are mainly closely geared to the notion of the overwhelming importance of music drama.

A fresh battalion of English choreographers has arisen, following—approximately—the footsteps of that select band who created so many staggering works of dance art in our rich period of the mid-thirties. To what extent the ballets of, among others, Helpmann, Cranko, Darrell, Carter, Morrice, Rodrigues and, most importantly, MacMillan may yet prove to be an advance of the choreographic craft is not yet wholly clear. A big factor influencing this hypothetical development is the degree to which the classical-balletic style of choreography has, everywhere in the West, been affected by other forms of theatre dance.

However much the supporters of the orthodox ballet may deny its value, Modern Dance in both its Central European and its American forms has made vast contributions to the world of light and lyric entertainment—very specifically in the field of what is erroneously called 'musical comedy'. Modern Dance grew up at a time when ballet had not become firmly implanted in the American soil. For a variety of racial, cultural and social reasons, this kind of dance (stressing Content rather than Form more clearly than does ballet) perfectly fitted the needs of American choreo-graphers with something to say. All of them, unlike their European counterparts, have been living in an atmosphere of Modern Dance all their lives. This has moulded their approach to all dance problems, whether their individual training has embraced classical ballet, ethnic, folk, modern styles—or an amalgam of many of them.

Now we have reached 'Modern Ballet', a trade-and-technical term for a kind of dancing which uses people trained in both Modern and Classical; today, a training in jazz and its variants can take the place of the Modern

Dance tuition. This is the basic movement equipment that today's American choreographers need as a minimum from all their performers. This new genre, plus the American style of Modern and of traditional ballet, are freely used to support the choreography serving the still-ascendant 'musical show'—the most popular form of Western theatrical entertainment of our time.

Both the European and the American schools of Modern Dance were as much under economic pressures as were the ballet groups during the forty-odd years of this survey. The Moderns gave to their side of our dance renaissance their kind of short, fast-actioned, one-acter. Knowing of, but often ignoring, Fokine's principles, they found, nevertheless, that they could not jettison them completely—or there could have been no impactive weight in their ballets and dances. Usually we find, on analysing much of their work, that they clung firmly to the first three principles; and quite often they disregarded altogether the fifth principle (on neither music nor *décor* being of greater importance than the dancing).

At this moment in dance history we are faced with a situation in which the popularity of ballet is forcing its impresarios (and here I do not exclusively mean the commercial boys who *have* to make their fifteen per cent. somehow) to devise more and more tricks to keep on selling a commodity which, by its nature, was never meant for assembly-line methods of manufacture and which, at its best, needs a sympathetic and fairly intelligent audience.

The economic organisation of ballet in any country is a complex of State money, commercial backing, nepotism and small-scale power politics—in France, in Russia, in America, and in England. Yet the basic conditions for an effective continuity of ballet are the same anywhere; there must be at the top of things one main company, a fountainhead with an academy attached, this academy supposedly setting standards, training a high-level type of performer, supplying a regular flow of dancers to the main, and other, companies. In every case it lives, and only continues to live, because it receives a State grant. The ballet theatres of every city in the world from Vienna to Valparaiso, from Nanking to New Orleans would go out of business within twenty-four hours if their government backing were cut off. Somehow, somewhere, smaller companies exist by receiving donations from rich patrons, from commercial bodies, or by a well-organised system of alternating tours with films and television engagements. Many of the odder developments in the ballet world of the West during the post-war period have been caused by financial stresses and compromises—mergers, changes of artistic direction, flashy productions aimed at insensitive audiences, overworked star-name dancers, etc., etc.

The analysis, so far, of this tumultuous achievement of fifty years suggests to me that Fokine's principles are still the valid basis for most ballet-making. Whether their exploitation for fifty years is now showing that they have come to the end of their usefulness seems to me highly debatable. The new methods of approach that such choreographers as Tudor, Balanchine, Petit, Robbins, MacMillan—to list the most dynamically active or ideologically most progressive—have shown to be workable, suggest that it is not yet possible to claim that Fokine's ideas are outworn.

The five principles of Fokine have often been mishandled sadly, to save a lazy choreographer from hard work; they have certainly been many times betrayed even when given lip-service. Yet we find these common-sense rules on which the ballet reformation of our century has been built are still viable, still artistically flexible enough for nearly every imaginable subject and its treatment. Most important—they are still a splendid discipline of the kind that choreographers need as they grope towards perfection of achievement.

# III

# *English Ballet*

# English Ballet

## (i) THE SCENE SURVEYED

EXCERPT FROM *Ballet Here and Now*

Neither the arts nor the sciences nor, indeed, any kind of intense human activity can be sectioned off into watertight and totally separate divisions; there is no such thing as a 'period' (e.g. the Elizabethan Era, the Counter-Reformation, the Industrial Revolution, the Romantic Age, etc., etc.) complete in itself. All activities spill over into the future and all of them have been influenced and shaped by the past. When we realise this fluid nature of the historical process we guard ourselves from over-simplifying our judgments. So we may talk of an 'early period' of English Ballet of our century, but it is impossible to say where it turned into the 'middle period'; we cannot pretend that already we can see the total shape of ballet developments in our time—even those that happened five or ten years ago.

Our early period covers the years in which the activities of Marie Rambert and Ninette de Valois began and the middle period can be estimated as those years in which swift expansions and growths were taking place; I would be reluctant to state that we have yet arrived at a final—or finalising—stage in our twentieth-century balletic growth. What is sure is that now, since about 1957-8, we have reached a point of hesitation.

Everything that occurred in our ballet in these thirty-odd years had been largely moulded by the shape and style of the ballet that came out of Russia in 1909; if for no other reason, because of the fact that its two chief architects, Rambert and de Valois, had both been subjected to its methods and came out of it with firm ideas about not only forming an English ballet—but also a future for English ballet.

Because we had a tradition of useful stage-dancing in this country, born of nineteenth-century pantomime and extravaganza, nourished in the Edwardian musical and somehow surviving the rigours of the 1914 war, there existed a foundation on which each of these remarkable women could erect a school, then a performing group, and finally create a theatre-company. By now, we have exploited everything that the native scene

41

could provide (including all the notions that native-born choreographers and directors could evolve) and we have had thirty years of strong, often successful growth. Now we are at a moment of stasis. We cannot, Nelson-like, turn a blind eye and pretend that this over-rapid development has not produced some evil as well as splendid results.

If our system of ballet is carried on into the future on the lines on which it is now operated, then I think we are heading fast for artistic sterility, then decline. But there can be no going back—or if we do think we can live on by repeating the formulas that started our ballet rebirth, then we are admitting that all we have done since 1926 has been to create a carbon copy of the Diaghilev method. We seem to have shown by now that nothing more can be achieved by following that path.

Why do I see that the point about 1957 can be identified as a position of stasis? Let us summarise what happened in the thirty years before. Quite simply: we began a minor ballet renaissance, modelled on the methods of Diaghilev. We bred choreographers in large numbers; we created a wholly new style of ballet at the Mercury; at Sadler's Wells we had a company capable of making interesting revivals of old 'classics' and a cautious amount of new ballet. We found an incredible supply of natural dance talent and trained it so that it could do full justice to our own kind of ballets. Although we could not match French or Russian achievement in the fields of designing and composing, we produced a few significant artists who had something rich to contribute to our ballet.

Nowhere else was there so genuine an interest—even though among only a small section of the populace—in ballet, as there was here in the 1930s. Between 1935 and 1940 (when war conditions abruptly upset everything) there were, at different times, twenty ballet companies active here.

All this did not happen because of fashion or wealth or because ruthless egomaniacs wanted something and somebody to control. It expressed the fact that we here were making an absolutely unique phase in ballet history: we quite literally—in relation to the size of our population—had more creative choreographers, lively dancers, competent musicians, adventurous designers than had been known anywhere else in the world. From their beginnings in the mid-twenties, the companies brought to birth by Rambert and de Valois had, by September 1939, created over one hundred original English ballets and had also revived works of Petipa, Fokine, Nijinsky.

The system had its financial difficulties, but basically things were kept going because the companies played short seasons or groups of intermittent performances, and the dancers could engage themselves in commercial work (revue, film, pantomime, summer shows) for a living. There was little strict unionisation then and often a ballet would be staged because dancers, teachers, supporters and staff would between them make costumes, paint scenery, rehearse one another, and so on.

Up to 1939 one was aware of a ballet world which, though only recently evolved, had won the respect of other theatre professionals, of most artists in other fields. There might be some balletgoers who followed the snobbism of the time and thought that the only ballet worth serious interest was that supplied by foreign companies visiting West End theatres; but there was a hard core audience faithfully supporting all that went on in the Mercury and at Sadler's Wells.

Inside ten years we produced, guided and pushed into maturity such creators as Frederick Ashton, Antony Tudor, Andrée Howard, Ninette de Valois, Frank Staff, Walter Gore. And what other group in any country can show so much variety of subject and style in their accumulated works? In the last twelve months before the war broke out, three valuable things had taken place. Both Ballet Rambert and the Sadler's Wells Ballet had been abroad, showed our products, and established that our new system of ballet was no mere flash in the pan: Antony Tudor, our greatest choreographer, had finally broken away from both Rambert and de Valois and set up a company which, artistically, was the biggest thing that English ballet had to show: de Valois' company had re-created versions of four nineteenth-century 'classics', culminating in a fifth—*The Sleeping Beauty* —in February, 1939.

Our whole new ballet system had by then an artistic strength as vital as that which Diaghilev's enterprise had shown in its first phase—the Golden Epoch of 1909 to 1914. No matter what the war did, we should have found a means of consolidating and developing this peculiarly English achievement at the war's end. We failed to do this, and in my view, set in motion in 1946 certain trends which have weakened the general artistic potential and have involved us in a mess of compromises over money, prestige, propaganda, artistic policies, training methods—and so on—from which the entire English ballet system suffers heavily.

The Arts Council, which was a larger version of the wartime C.E.M.A., came into being after the war and it inevitably embraced among its advisers and directors and power-manipulators those who wished for the prestige of Britain having a great National Ballet. It was not difficult to make good artistic propaganda out of the decision to take over the Royal Opera House, remove it from purely commercial handling, and make it the location of a National Ballet, soon to be partnered by a National Opera.

At this point in history, when the circumstances could have been used to launch English ballet into as powerful a position as Diaghilev had held

in 1909, we made our big miscalculation. Of course we needed a central academy for training, we needed a big showcase theatre, we needed a mechanism which would feed ballet both to the provinces and also, ultimately, the benighted foreigner. These problems, however, required thrashing out with the purest sort of artistic consciousness, in an atmosphere of clear integrity; we needed to apply every lesson that could have been learned from our marvellous adventure of the 1930s. We should also have seen the need to learn all that was possible from the methods by which the French, Italians, Russians, Danes, etc., had coped with the problems of establishing and running complex State theatrical systems. Could anyone, inside or outside our ballet system, have pleaded that breakneck speed was the most desirable attribute? That, somehow, we were going to lose national prestige by not having a National Ballet in being within a year of war's ending? Certainly not. A body of inquiry using all the talents of those who had imagined, worked for, sustained and assisted our ballet's rebirth should have thrashed out the problems calmly, logically, wisely; and then set up a guiding directorate which embodied everyone who could give valuable service. No financial condition was so difficult that we could not have maintained all our existing ballet companies in going order for another year or two, preparatory to launching our National Ballet and its Theatre with a workable programme, a live policy, and a company (or companies) recruited from the whole field of English talent.

I do not think I ask too much in wanting—as I wanted at that time—all our ability, ideas, talents, to be utilised for the glory and advancement of the idea of English ballet. But Fate—which is another name for pressure-groups, prestige-seekers, propagandists—willed otherwise. The Sadler's Wells company became by a stroke of the pen, not by artistic leadership, the English National Ballet.

Even during the rest of the 1940s and into the early 1950s our ballet system looked fairly healthy and vital. The post-war years of readjustment still found people spending money on culture to the same extent as in the period 1939-45 and by 1947 London had come to be the world's ballet centre. We had at least seven companies active and the opening up of international channels of communication led to a vast increase in the international exchange of theatre attractions. If the English were so crazy about ballet—so the commercial impresarios must have reasoned—then they will pay to see anything, everything. During the first post-war decade we were visited by ballet and dance companies from every nation which had anything respectable to show. Probably too late for their lessons to be taken in, we finally saw the finer achievements of American, French, Danish and Russian ballet. If our directors and choreographers have been willing to apply new ideas, new treatments, new policies derived from what these national groups had achieved, it has been done in piecemeal fashion, intermittently, by fits and starts.

What went wrong, in my view, was that about 1958 the Royal Ballet's policy had obviously finally become unworkable. Unworkable, that is, if we want the organisation to be as culturally important as was the Imperial Ballet in Russia seventy years ago and as the Royal Danish Ballet is today to the Danish way of life.

Since the first American visit in 1949 the company has gradually sunk deeper into a system of compromises (largely concerning money, space and timetables) which preclude it being a top-class, healthy, State ballet organisation. The obvious *facts* of the present method of 'working compromises' are: (1) that the company gives over-long seasons and too many performances for a high level of theatricality to emerge continuously; (2) that the company's propaganda overstates the value of nineteenth-century classical ballets which are too few in number and imprecise in structure to form a standard for measuring all balletic achievement; (3) the organisation has failed to make a training system which sympathetically embraces the interests equally of choreographers, dancers, composers, and designers; (4) the company works in a theatre, shared by an opera company, which lacks adequate staging, storage and rehearsal facilities. It has been claimed elsewhere that all this would be rectified if the Opera House grant were increased. I doubt this.

What is the clear achievement of our National Ballet since it took up residence at Covent Garden? The talent of Margot Fonteyn, restricted from full blossoming by wartime activities (eight shows a week, forty-eight weeks a year) erupted fully in a series of carefully—but not carefully enough—revived classics, and in many new roles devised by Ashton. Rightfully she assumed her place among the world's dozen top ballerinas. Ashton, returning from the war, quickly found his old form, then went beyond it, with *Symphonic Variations, Scènes de Ballet, Ondine, La Fille mal gardée,* and re-creations on old scenarios and scores of *Cinderella, Daphnis and Chloë, Sylvia, Les Deux Pigeons.* The best of the pre-war ballets have been given short revivals, the classics re-worked, re-rehearsed and re-produced. Prestige visits have been paid to most of Europe's leading cities and profitable, but artistically sterilising, trips made to America. Whatever other results they achieve—and the most recent was admittedly valuable in earning money to make good some operatic deficiencies—they have, in a roundabout and nicely logical way, helped the

British taxpayer to enlarge the bank accounts of the company's foreign impresarios.

The Royal Ballet's school has been expanded and is in liaison with most good schools in the country and British territories overseas. Most lively potential dance talent gets channelled towards it and, consequently, the company has a large proportion of dancers from Africa (white, naturally), Australia, New Zealand, Canada. Although the Arts Council grant is used to maintain the company, some payments are made to help the school, and it has been given a number of dance scholarships to dispose of by various commercial and local government bodies. A prodigious if usually badly co-ordinated system of propaganda, working on dozens of levels, has sold the public the notion that 'English Ballet' means the company at Covent Garden and its ancillary activities.

Externally, and possibly even internally, all ideas about the shape, size, policy and methods of the Royal Ballet are supposed to have an affinity with the system of the old-established State ballets of various European countries . . . but with differences of detail. Each of these systems— Russian, Danish, French, to quote the more solid—has taken literally centuries to make a working method embracing all its affairs. Such questions as choice of repertoire, grading and promotion of dancers, duration of training and its curriculum, mode of discipline, system of recruitment, scales of pay and rewards, holidays, protection in sickness, etc., have taken time to work out and have been the hard work of genera-tions of cautious administrators, managers and directors. The important question of a method whereby one person (under advice and guidance), or a panel, has the power to hire-and-fire, to promote or demote dancers, to choose interesting talents as choreographic-and-other creators, has been solved only after scrupulous argument, suggestions and persuasion.

Here we seem to order these matters differently. True, a Trust governs Covent Garden in a general way and certainly there are lots of advisers (even if only known as names on an Arts Council panel), but the total effect appears to be that we have a National Ballet run by an omnipotent director whose word is law on all matters.

One may never hear of a dancer being unjustly dismissed, but there is no method of appeal known to the world outside Covent Garden whereby a dancer may protest against a directorial decision. All dancers are on one-year contracts with no compulsory renewal clause; whatever rate of pay they get is won by personal bargaining and there is no pension scheme. Perhaps most of this seems not only inevitable, but good; and is justified by the methods whereby we created a National Ballet overnight, and by the size of the Arts Council grant . . . always allegedly too small.

In a lecture not long ago, Dame Ninette de Valois gave a précis of what the Royal Ballet had done, was doing, and was intended to do. Emphasis was laid on the fact that the 'English School has now absorbed classicism', and that it is now 'creating its own interpretations of traditional classical ballets'. Two notions for the future are the re-establishment of the full-length ballet (as a swing of the pendulum against the past fifty years' preoccupation with the one-acter?), and the belief that our choreographers can begin to find workable source material in English folk-dance lore.

One must agree that classical works from an earlier epoch have value; the difficulty is that we have far too few of them to build a wide catalogue of reference against which we must measure our modern achievement. One must also agree that we must breed dancers who deploy a good classical style; the trouble is that definitions of that style vary somewhat, and the means of inducing that style vary absolutely among all the acceptable dance teachers both within and outside the Royal Ballet system.

In ballet, 'classics' are not classics in the sense that great works of music, painting, literature, architecture are; they are *contemporary re-interpretations* of what we like to think the originals looked and felt like. If classical style in dancing—which should be a pure, lyric and noble mode of presenting the human body—means anything, then it must embody every freshness in deploying the human body that a choreographer of invention can discover (this, working inside the convention of the system of movement based on five foot positions and with the extra female convention of dancing on the point). Such notions as a more plastic use of arms and torso, the interplay of curves and masses between a pair of partnering bodies, the use of adaptations from old folk-dance steps, controlled and related uses of speed in movement, slow motion and even stasis—these are the additions of this century's 'neo-classicism'. They mark the common fund of choreographic invention and discovery since Petipa and Ivanov, and much of it has been used in ballets by the later Fokine, Massine, Tudor and Balanchine.

How can it be 'classicism', as a performing style, if frozen into a convention which had been totally worked out by 1841?

The sort of lively repertoire a good National Ballet should command ought to hold examples of every variant of nineteenth-century classicism (i.e. let us dig into the archives and find what Mérante, Ivanov, Perrot, Paul Taglioni, Petipa put into some of the ballets that went on the shelf in 1840, 1860, 1870, 1880, etc.). It should encompass works showing the best of neo-classicism and ballets based on lively use of all kinds of social and folk movement activity (ballroom styles, ensemble folk dances, primitive patterns such as still validate folk dancing in the Arab, Mongol,

Negro, Indian worlds); and all the good things that generations of tap, cabaret and exhibition dancers have worked on.

And so, not very indirectly, this brings us back to dance-education in nineteenth-century Russia, where encyclopaedic methods of tuition were merely the first plank of the platform on which the choreographer would, later, build. We shall *not* make a vital form of either 'our own interpretation of traditional classics', or a good use of neo-classicism, until we train our teachers and our potential dance-creators in a method as comprehensive as inquiry, research and imagination can devise. I find absolutely no evidence whatever that the training methods for teachers, choreographers or mere dancers in our National Ballet system, nor the production methods at Covent Garden, nor the general artistic guidance of individual dancers in the Royal Ballet School, are moving towards any such ideal. All our female dancers have been totally indoctrinated with the ambition to be 'a classical ballerina'; to them, modern ballets are just so many *hors d'oeuvres* on which to whet the appetite for the great dishes of Odette-Odile, Aurora, Giselle, the Sugar Plum Fairy and, a long way behind, Swanilda.

Of course we could find some old classics if we wanted to. When Sergueev left Russia he brought scores and choreographic scripts (in Stepanov notation, which can be fairly easily taught) of more than twenty ballets. Out of these he produced the first Sadler's Wells classics; the others ought to include some not abysmally banal as regards plot, music and choreographic structure; and we have here among his documents at least five which still survive in today's Soviet repertoire: *Raymonda\*, The Humpbacked Horse, Esmeralda, Don Quixote,* and *La Bayadère\**.

The Royal Ballet tours because it must, to justify the Arts Council grant coming out of all Britain's taxpayers' pockets; it tours abroad for prestige purposes (and, in America, to win a pittance for the credit side of the ledger). But this touring is done on a basis of losing 'so much money' inevitably; whereas the only near-competition—London Festival Ballet and Ballet Rambert—tour to try to make ends meet, or merely to keep going. The folly is that, without any joint planning, they financially (and possibly artistically) cut one another's throats when they follow one another too quickly in Birmingham, Aberdeen, Hull, etc.

But for the sake of preserving the actual style and dance-quality of the ballets, and to allow the dancers to give truly creative performances, no company should tour for more than, say, six continuous weeks. The

*Through Nureyev's influence, single acts of these two ballets have been put on at Covent Garden. The London Festival Ballet have added *Don Quixote* to their repertory.

simplest sort of planning could allocate a touring schedule for all the companies, to cover Great Britain, and save money, nerves, and wear-and-tear on apparatus in prodigious quantities.

A far bigger miscalculation (or possibly total absence of calculation?) in the planning of the National Ballet's aims in 1945, was the perpetuation of the mad, bad idea that companies can live healthily on non-stop performance schedules. The State Ballets in Europe have an annual season lasting about seven, perhaps eight, months and ballet is usually given, at most, thrice weekly. Dancers get holidays long enough to relax and refresh themselves, to meet new people, to find that there is a world where people talk of something other than dancing. Half the personal problems as well as their professional ones affect English dancers as intensely as they do because they live too much in a closed world peopled only by dancers.

When, as a further solemn thought, we consider that the Covent Garden company averaged over one period of five years a fraction over four performances weekly (discounting Sundays off) can we delude ourselves that its condition is healthy? Ballerinas, of course, share the top roles and appear sparingly in such works; but can a cast performing at this rate (with about thirty short ballets in mixed programmes interpolated with the bigger works) be supposed to give creative performances—with the character fully felt and correctly projected? If the *corps-de-ballet* frequently don't appear to be dying on their pretty feet, they as often as not seem to be going through a well-numbed routine which lacks both total personalities and total uniformity of pattern.

If it is believed that such feats of endurance and carthorse labouring are due to the inadequacy of the financial system, then it is high time we re-examined the finances with a view to spending them on fewer and possibly better performances. Instead of helping us to create a splendidly alive National Ballet such methods of performance are simply holding back the work that should be carried out.

And while the odd few hundreds of thousands are being split in a more sensible way, could we not summon up the ingenuity (and the small sum of cash needed) to create a really experimental unit where sets of dancers and musicians and choreographers, in a method of rotation, could work simply as a try-out mechanism? A ballet laboratory where, without cruel pressures of time, means and money, our apprentices could learn, or teach one another, the crafts they ought to know.

These few problems are only part of the unsatisfactory state of our balletic affairs; the revising of the repertoire; the fresh examination of what 'classicism' means and how to acquire it; the cessation of over-strenuous tours; the beginning of training creative artists by first making them good craftsmen . . . these are problems of such urgency that they require immediate examination—but by a body of people from our ballet world whose minds are not firmly fixed in the notion that the Pangloss estimate is the only possible one.

And still other questions arise: how is success measured? Is a ballet 'good' because seven leading critics (out of how many?) enthuse over it? Yet the general public won't accept it? Or is it a 'success' because the management believes in it and keeps it in repertoire despite thin houses? Are the management right to blame critics (whom they freely accuse of ignorance) if ballets don't succeed? Should the public be blamed because it has too willingly swallowed the trashy propaganda which paints all ballet as a big glamorous adventure? So that in the theatre this public cannot accept any ballet which does not happen to look like *Swan Lake*? Over recent years too much of ballet's own publicity—that put out by the companies' own publicity 'experts'—has given a bogus picture of what ballet is for, what it is about, what it can give; so that an entire new public has been drawn into watching ballet which comes to see the ballerina being a ballerina—and not being a woman creating a theatrical characterisation.

All this sad appraisal, which I consider a careful reading of the evidence and by no means exaggerated, leads me back again and again to the central problem; which is, how can we expect any creative work of enduring, even solid, quality when we fail to train dancers and choreographers in a proper understanding of what this delicate art can do and be?

We have some wonderful dance talent, a lot of which I suspect feels that it gets too little encouragement and moral support from the managements as well as the critics. We have fifty major problems on our collective hands, if we really think we want to make our ballet an expression of whatever is, at this moment, the native genius. All our fine achievement arose because we began the work under conditions wherein people of vision and courage worked and fought hard for a splendid idea. Success—both the good and bad kinds—came too fast; and our folly has been that, since 1945, we have rushed ahead too fast without troubling to see in which direction we were supposed to be moving.

Now, worse off than the Red Queen in *Through the Looking-Glass* we don't merely run fast in order to stay in the same place—we are running like mad things and—artistically—are slipping back all the time.

An older English ballet perished under the hot breath of the war of 1914-18, and from its ashes, with an incantation learned from Diaghilev and Fokine, we created a new kind of English ballet. Must it perish, too, strangled in the hot, careless embrace of those who care more for success than for artistic achievement?

But I believe that every one of our problems can be solved, with a lot of clear thinking and unselfishness. We need more money and even more fresh ideas and methods, in dance schools, in theatres, in the choreographer's workshops, in the critics' studies. But it needs splendid liaison all round the ballet world; and who is there experienced, wise, and respected enough (and still vigorous enough) to give the rest of us a lead?

TACTICS WITHOUT STRATEGY
From *The Daily Telegraph*, 4 October, 1967.
More new ballets have been made so far this year than in any comparable period; some find a place in touring repertories, most fade quietly out of knowledge after a handful of performances. There is no evidence that a startling new choreographic talent is visible, yet the general picture is encouraging.

For the young of the ballet world are trying hard (sometimes much too hard!) to express themselves, not always selfishly, through new dance notions.

The Ballet Rambert's rebirth last year as primarily a "discovering" organisation has shown the company avidly trying out new British and old French and American choreographers. The Royal Ballet early this year discovered a whole nest of aspirant creators in its midst and put on a programme at Guildford; soon after, London Festival Ballet gave its embryo choreographers a field day.

Within a few days the London Contemporary Dance Group will stage its first crop of novelties; these will be the fruit of the setting up of the first school in this country teaching the free-form style of Martha Graham. Including the not-despicable efforts of the best of the non-professional groups, I reckon that by Christmas I shall have seen a hundred new ballets this year, in and around London.

It is highly desirable that English ballet should buzz with so much liveliness, but unless some kind of coherent planning for the future is applied the value of all this intense activity will be small.

For in no instance among all these "ballet workshops," "trial programmes." and "choreographic experiments" is there any overall plan for a campaign to conquer and consolidate new dance territory.

These "soldiers" make little forays into strange country, win small victories—then find themselves back at their starting point because they have no method of consolidating.

There is a sign now that some managerial talents are seeing—at last!— the desirability of a method that can give the embryo choreographer a useful weapon for his future campaigns. It is not much use his having ideas unless he also has a minimal knowledge of craft, and the crafts-manship for choreography is not only untaught in any of our ballet schools, it is largely unformulated.

This happens simply because successful choreographers up to now have had to learn the hard way, by trial and error, through their own teaching and self-teaching, and by dancing in other people's ballets. Understandably, though unfortunately, nobody is more opposed to setting up the teaching of craftsmanship than the successful choreographers.

Yet the devising of a basic craft course would clarify for the student-choreographer certain first principles of ballet-making. There is no question of anyone learning this difficult business in "six easy lessons"; the basic guidance would teach beginners an alphabet, where at present they must learn their letters by listening to others.

The necessary elements are few and could be taught in a basic course, as follows:

> Learning to play an instrument enough to get a skeletal notion of the *structure* of music (the piano or recorder would serve well enough).
>
> Learning to read a simple score and going on to understand scores of more complexity.
>
> Studying movement through anatomical instruction—not just as dancing in a classroom.
>
> Elements of logic and geometry to find how to use all the dimensions of a stage.
>
> Training in the simple principles of mathematics and optics, to learn *how* and *why* colour, lighting and form contribute to theatrical effect.

Such a course would not involve a complex academic apparatus; it could be operated in three teaching units flexibly arranged so that students could move from section to section as they found necessary. These three units would comprise a practical music course, a study-scheme using a wide range of illustrative matter to cover the geometry, mathematics, optics and anatomy, and a historical survey.

This would not guarantee that any individual student would ever create a masterpiece of ballet—but it would avoid the errors that occur in every trial group I have watched for years.

It could end such existing bad practices as using music of unsuitable dynamic structure; décor of too great a complexity; lighting which creates neither a dramatic nor an aesthetic effect; movement styles unfitted for a particular subject, and dance patterns too complex or repetitive to have any meaning.

Which of our more advanced ballet schools or companies will enter 1968 with some such scheme ready to go into operation? A year's trial would cost less than a one-act ballet for Covent Garden.

A TIME OF CRISIS (1968)
Not previously published
The last great admitted crisis in the history of ballet affected every kind of theatrical dancing and also had indirect influence upon many kinds of social dance. This critical turning-point, which came around the years 1890-1906, let loose influences which have not yet been fully accommodated into the art and science of ballet and so, in more senses than one, ballet is still in a state of crisis. (This is one reason why I find it of continually absorbing interest.)

That turning-point was really a series of separate events spread over a number of years and an important one was the system of iconoclastic ideas, and the dances illustrating them, displayed by both Loie Fuller and Isadora Duncan. At the time there was fermenting in St Petersburg a group of young men, consisting mainly of Benois, Fokine, Diaghilev, Filosofov, Bakst, all eager to change the face of ballet. How far they succeeded is to be seen in what ensued over the whole world of ballet after the Diaghilev company appeared in Paris in 1909.

Artistic innovations do not strike total sympathy even out of a culturally alert public unless some seeds of propaganda, whether deliberate or unconscious, have already been sown. The notion of the absolute basic importance of the art of dancing (not just ballet) had been the concern of many poets, painters and thinkers active in Paris and London since the 1870s. Much of their thought and utterance had served to re-emphasise (what is regularly being overlooked) that dancing is a primary art and also is probably the most valuable autoanalytic activity in which mankind engages.

Within those few years that covered the careers of Duncan and Fuller (both Americans), the choreographic career of Fokine, and the impresario's career of Diaghilev there emerged not only the renaissance of ballet as a serious art, but also the birth of the notion of the Free Dance, instigated mainly by the ideas of Fuller and Duncan. In Europe it was based largely on the theories of Laban and Wigman; in America it grew from the parallel activities of Ruth St Denis and Ted Shawn. From their school emerged Graham, and from the formulas and practices of this trio came that incentive which stirred dozens of revolutionaries who by teaching, preaching, dancing and choreographing created the whole of America's Modern Dance.

As a consequence of these two theatrical disturbances, the questioning of previous values, the endless probing about aesthetics, the spreading of the boundaries of technique and expressiveness that followed for ballet— even in Soviet Russia in its earliest years—were of a magnitude comparable with the other 20th century artistic upheavals in painting, architecture, music, literature and dramatic form.

The revival of ballet here was a true rebirth after only a brief quiescence, for our native ballet of the late 19th century had retained its unique vitality and aesthetic until the changing conditions of the period 1914-18 swept it from the theatre. Many of those involved in our renaissance as choreographers, directors, dancers, were workers with the Diaghilev Company at different times. They included Marie Rambert, Ninette de Valois, Tamara Karsavina, Lydia Sokolova, Lydia Lopokova, Stanislas Idzikovsky and Anton Dolin—all of their ideas much conditioned by their work in that company.

The lasting impact from Diaghilev was made up of the setting up of a sort of ballet that re-established the choreographer as the essential creator; the invention of the practicality as well as of the artistic value of the one-act ballet; the stimulation of co-operation between like-minded choreographer, composer and designer; the staging on a Europe-wide platform of the new choreographic practices of Fokine and, later, of Massine, Nijinska and Balanchine.

We can look back on many of the works of that period with the superiority of hindsight and possibly see them as naive in music, old-fashioned in scenario, obvious in décor and melodramatic in mime; but they were, for that time, the epitomes of the one-act ballet form, and that has become the "normal" ballet of today. We might also reflect that the best examples from the Diaghilev repertoire offered a kind of visual beauty of complete originality, not created before in any theatre style.

All that the Diaghilev venture had shown (together with the valuable but differently scaled work of Pavlova with her own company) was raw material, incentive, shining example and stimulation for that wave of choreographers that sprang—almost literally out of the paving stones of London—when Miss de Valois (an Irishwoman) and Madame Rambert (a Pole), at the Old Vic and the Mercury, gave English ballet to the English in the mid-1920s.

Those young creators, comprising de Valois herself, Ashton, Howard, Tudor, Staff and Gore are part of the history of dance creation; a new generation which was largely moulded through experience of the works of that founding sextet now forms the spearhead of native choreographic endeavour: its best known names are MacMillan, Cranko, Carter, Morrice and Darrell. Recollecting, comparing and analysing all the splendid, horrified, heroic, depressed, uplifted and shocked reactions I have had to hundreds of performances of all these people's ballets emphasises that this chaos of impressions exactly reflects the chaotic state of English ballet today. This fact is less a cause for regret than an incentive for more questions about the actual health of our ballet now, for chaos means instability and this at least signifies life and therefore some sort of health. This chaotic condition has in fact lasted since we founded our ballet nearly forty years ago.

Let me try to render some sort of account of what I find in the picture of our ballet activity. There are those who would say that merely to have gone on existing for forty years is a sign of good health and that we should not worry about the evidence of growing pains and youthful blemishes. I am more interested in knowing whether our forty-year-old is by now an adult creature enjoying perfect health and happiness—or not: and, if not, to discuss why.

The biggest asset—and, comparatively, it is a bigger asset than even the Russian and American ballet systems have today—is the actual quantity of pupils, teachers, dancers, producers and technicians, musicians and designers; for a nation of our size we have produced more choreographers per acre than France has produced novelists, Russia mystics, and Italy painters.

Schools of several grades turn out hundreds of finished students yearly who have often (but not always) received, as well as ballet instruction, tuition in mime, musical theory, presentation, Modern Dance and folk dancing. For various personal reasons many people in the past thirty years have put up enough money to start more than thirty English ballet companies, most of which died quickly. A few of them lived a useful and healthy life for a year or two, the benefits being that a few dancers got chances to prove (or disprove) their talent and some budding choreographers put out one or two faint or occasionally vigorous blossoms.

The most remarkable single aspect of all this period has been that there was no time at which one central company—however big, however well-run, however artistically vital—has dominated the whole picture. In those countries where ballet was long-established all activity centred on, or was directed by, the head of the national or state ballet system.

Our advantage has been to have this multiplicity of small groups, for however awful some have been, it has meant that choreographers, dancers, designers of true daring, were enabled to work out some part of their destinies. Because of their indisputable size, artistic leanings and comparative antiquity, the Royal Ballet (earlier the Sadler's Wells Ballet) and the Ballet Rambert have produced or stimulated a high proportion of our wealth of talent; but the other (and usually smaller) companies have made some contributions of value. This has meant that the total richness of all our ballet activity is more diversified than that of any other country.

This very richness of material, both raw and experimental, is paradoxically the weakness of English ballet today; we now have too many companies operating in a world too small for their *artistic* health, all competing for what money is available and also for the livelier examples of dancing or choreographic talent.

State subsidy plus box-office receipts enable some companies to go on performing and regularly creating new works; the smaller the subsidy the more precarious the company and certainly the fewer new ballets get made. The companies lacking subsidy run on backing from well-wishers prepared to lose their shirts, or on hand-to-mouth loans which are repaid (or partly repaid) out of next season's takings. Some companies have started on too little money and go into a state of suspension when the bookings fail: the dancers have to disperse to earn their bread elsewhere.

Some may think that it would be immensely simplified if the State subsidy were increased and every company given a calculated sum to allow it to go into operation with the expectancy of making its running costs out of box-office takings. But no government anywhere would (or ought to be expected to) provide blank cheques simply because yet another group of assorted ballet folk think that they have a "good idea" for a company.

What this financial turmoil means really is that the recently won fight to get State recognition has been a victory for the big battalions; the smaller squadrons receive sums helping with only a part of their expenses. The other companies have been lucky to find private backers willing to take a chance on ballet rather than on buying post-Impressionist paintings. (Of course, Diaghilev had to do exactly this after his Imperial subsidy ran out once he was launched in Paris).

I am not privy to the imaginings of any English ballet director on any matter, but I suspect that those running the larger groups deplore the existence of the others, for they take up some of the State money: their repertoires sometimes overlap those of the Establishment; and often these companies are (disgracefully) too daring. Those running the small companies look enviously at the scale of help given by the taxpayer to their bigger brethren.

In all this complex of cash, imagination, power-politics, ambition and unhappiness there is no true co-ordination, no sharing of top-class talents or available markets, no basic agreement on how each section could find a worthwhile place in a *general pattern of English ballet*. Managements may invite one another's directors and star dancers to important first nights, but these are occasions for displaying their own shop-windows, rather than friendly gestures of respect.

Touring companies, each drawing Arts Council subsidy, are booked into the same city together, or so close to one another that there is little audience response to the second comer.

The secret ambition of every student in a dance academy in this country is to get into the Royal Ballet. Why? Not because it is the most artistically exciting organisation to work in—far from it—but because it is a safer and a more prestige-making job . . . and with the extra interest of all those trips to America, and the making of TV appearances, and a working year of more than forty-five paid weeks. This, of course, has led to an attitude among young dancers and final-year students which denigrates the value of the smaller companies. Much of this attitude (as well as most of the widespread and frequently inaccurate values for ballet) has grown out of the popular image created out of propaganda. Needless to say much of this propaganda has been disseminated by people associated with This or That company, and equipped with a whole armoury of axes ready for grinding.

There is no single person to be blamed for this: rather, in my view, a majority of critics and popularisers have over the years jointly created this distorted view of what ballet is, what it can give, what it can do. This state arises partly because a critic of ballet can begin (and go on for a long time) with no basic qualifications, unlike the critic of literature, music or painting, who must be well informed about the technique, history and aesthetics of his art to write usefully.

A wide collection of critics' notices on a new ballet or a revival will usually show a majority of views which take no heed of the balletic proportions of the work; it is liked (or disliked) because it gives a leading dancer a splendid or a less-than-splendid role, or because its brilliant décor hides its dull choreography, or because its novel theme and music cover up imperfect characterisation and dancing. Few ballets, of course, are perfect blendings of the essential elements; but too much of our criticism is a series of snap judgments on certain aspects of the production and not considered value-judgments on the entire creation—with assessments of dancing, scenario, sets, costumes, music *and* their choreographic fusion.

We have critics writing in responsible newspapers who work for ballet companies as teachers and lecturers, critics who work in administrative posts in ballet. This brand of critical writing together with the hearty propaganda in magazines and books has helped to create part of that ballet-image which stresses entertainment value and personality sensation but ignores the fact of the work of art.

Part of the value of a real critical system for any sort of theatre art is that the public is offered thirty or forty different opinions from sensitive, and sympathetic, (but different) critics, *none of them in any sort of friendly alliance with any one company.*

Both Royal Ballet companies, and London Festival Ballet, embrace the belief that revivals of 19th century ballets (of any quality or vintage) are what the public yearns for; this public appetite being wholly fostered by a publicity system which the managements have themselves created. The courage to press on continually creating new ballets as the essential condition for a vital art seems mostly lacking in our ballet system. An inevitable concomitant to this attitude has been a cautiousness in choosing choreographers and in giving them chances. They have to be self-trained, by dancing, teaching, and watching other people's ballets; we turn our backs on the notion of giving them a craftsman's equipment with which they could more confidently approach the effort of creation.

Perhaps much of what I have said seems a raking over of trivialities; my heartfelt wish is that there were less triviality in the thoughts and actions of a majority of those in charge of English ballet. But this state of affairs *does* exist—managements not knowing what the public wants (and doing no sort of research to find out); a wavering attitude towards the idea of making choreographers keep on working at new ballets; the mentality which cannot decide whether the ballerina counts as much as, more than, or less than the choreographer; most seriously, the fact that too many companies exist, considering the small amount of public money available, the little private backing that can be found, and the smallness of the market. Even in the boom period 1946-1954, if two important companies played simultaneously in London, at no performance were both houses full.

On the other hand: we have marvellous assets for a great resurgence of ballet which could give the art a vitality and topical sensibility as exciting as those that accompanied the early years of the Diaghilev venture, the first periods of de Basil, of the Blum-Fokine company.

No person is to blame, least of all any one individual involved in ballet, but all of us together are responsible for the confused picture of what ballet is. There is too little sensible liaison between companies, critics, and creative artists out of which they could mould an attitude compounded equally of respect for and understanding of each others' values, hopes and tasks. Eight companies does not spell "healthy competition"; it emphasises unhealthy competition, it is a situation in which the strong fight to become stronger and the weakest (not necessarily artistically, but financially) are driven to the wall. Yet all this feeling of tumultuous crisis, of chaos somehow being occasionally guided into order and coherence, does give to our ballet a part of its liveliness.

The situation needs a master figure, comparable with but wholly different from Diaghilev and with some of his taste, sympathy, knowledge, and worshipful attitude towards the arts of the theatre. Then, of course, once he began working we should have another really first-class crisis on top of us, but what a thrill that would provide! Think of the heads that (unfortunately only metaphorically) would roll!


## (ii) ANTONY TUDOR AND THE LONDON BALLET

The article 'An English Career' (the title has an ironic flavour
in retrospect) was serialised in *Dance Chronicle* in 1941/42.
It is partly valuable as first hand reporting of a unique occasion,
for Coton worked in a many-sided capacity for Tudor's London
Ballet during the period covered in this article; but the critical
points made in it about Tudor's neglect in pre-war England seem
totally valid in the perspective of the 1970s.

### ANTONY TUDOR: AN ENGLISH CAREER

The Ballet Rambert was housed at the Mercury Theatre from 1931 to 1940, and every English figure of any consequence to ballet danced, designed, played, painted or produced something during the winter weekend performances at Ladbroke Road throughout nine eventful years.

The two most significant choreographic talents thrown up in this period are Ashton and Tudor: both came to ballet late and each received valuable help and guidance from Marie Rambert. Both, as part of a process of artistic and technical development, passed out of her orbit and plunged into ballet production on a different scale from that to which they had been bound by the Mercury's microscopic stage and limited technical resources.

Whereas Ashton has acquired an international reputation chiefly from his work with Sadler's Wells Ballet, Tudor up to the outbreak of war had to be content to mount his work on small groups (save for his work on Covent Garden Opera Ballet) and never had the opportunity which Ashton has enjoyed of working inside a well organised theatre, operating on a fifty-two weeks-a-year basis—with skilled technicians, a first-rate musical director and a permanent orchestra at his disposal.

Up to September 1939 Tudor's works off the Mercury's experimental stage were only seen as part of the Ballet Rambert's West End seasons, or at the few performances given by the brilliant company of which he was choreographer and director—the London Ballet, founded in the autumn of 1938.

Antony Tudor did not make his first contact with ballet until well into his teens. It is a remarkable achievement that within a few short years he had learned enough of dance, music and stagecraft to put on his first experiment at the Mercury Theatre in November 1931. *Cross-Gartered* was a simple story of Malvolio's unsuccessful wooing of Olivia, told to Frescobaldi music.

Tudor was single-minded in his determination to master all that could be *learned* about ballet. After the first contact with Pavlova, which had inspired all his interest in the art, he assiduously studied literature and music at night schools, and saved out of his small salary to pay for dancing lessons. Very soon he reconstituted his entire living scheme to forward his chosen career. He gave up his outside employment and became secretary and stage manager of the Mercury Theatre. His days were filled with the study of dancing, acting, stagecraft and music: and reading, reading and reading.

He produced his next four ballets within two and a half years— *Lysistrata,* to Prokofiev music, and *Atalanta of the East* (Seelig) were both decorated by William Chappell, then a fellow-student and dancer at the Ballet Club, and were both produced between July 1932 and May 1933. The first work of any length was the three movement ballet to three parts of Gustav Holst's "Planets" Suite, produced in the mid-winter of 1934/35. Choosing Venus, Mars and Neptune, Tudor effected a close sympathy between the vigorous romantic music and the plasticity and dramatic poignancy of his choreographic forms. The décor of Hugh Stevenson helped tremendously, and was the first of a series of many felicitous collaborations.

Shortly after establishing himself as a choreographer, Tudor was in search of a wider field for his activities. He not unreasonably thought that our National Theatre of Ballet might one day be interested in his work, and during the 1934/35 winter season he was dancing with Sadler's Wells Ballet. It was during his attachment to this company that he created for the Ballet Rambert both *The Planets* and *The Descent of Hebe*. The uncertain reception that had been accorded his choreographic début was gradually amended to recognition of his outstanding ability by the time, in 1936, he produced the first of his two finest ballets. *Jardin aux Lilas,* like so many other ballet projects, began with a quite different idea from that which it embodied when completed. Originally there was to be a ballet based on a Finnish legend related in one of Aino Kallas' stories. But certain qualities of the story could not be conveyed successfully through the medium of ballet, and the libretto which now forms the basis of action was hammered out by Tudor in collaboration with certain friends. We must remember that all the Ballet Rambert's choreographers had a constant awareness of the limitations of their stage and its technical resources: all ideas of novel movement or lighting, and of extensive groupings have had to be generally somewhat amended between their first conception and their produced versions. Tudor no doubt contemplated working within those limits for some time to come.

He was fortunate in working amongst dancers who, on the whole, were keenly interested in his creations. The successful presentation of most of his ballets at their initial staging was, in great part, due to the high standards of dancing and acting which he demanded from the executants, who in their turn gave willingly. They gave because those of them who believed in the importance of ballet had an awareness of Tudor's unique style, a respect for his tremendous appetite for hard work, and a strong desire that ballets of such obvious merit as *The Planets, Descent of Hebe* and *Jardin aux Lilas* should succeed.

From time to time the Ballet Rambert presented a West End season of ballet in a larger theatre than their own. The growing public for ballet justified the risks involved in what, at an earlier date, might easily have been a financial disaster. At the beginning of 1937 English Ballet altogether appeared to be in a very healthy state. Since joining Sadler's Wells as a permanent choreographer-dancer, Ashton had produced *Les Rendezvous, Le Baiser de la Fée, Siesta, Apparitions* and *Nocturne,* a group representing some of the best works of one of his most fruitful periods. The Markova-Dolin Ballet, launched in December 1935, was still in action, with a repertory of indifferently produced classics and a few interesting new productions or revivals by Nijinska, Dolin and Wendy Toye. Andrée Howard had emerged as the Ballet Club's newest prodigy, coeval with Tudor, and had already achieved several ballets displaying an extraordinary flair for the creation of atmosphere.

The February 1937 season of the Ballet Rambert showed a remarkable collection of dancing talent, in twenty-four ballets, all (with the exception of Nijinsky's *Faune*) the achievement of choreographers unknown or undeveloped at Diaghilev's death. Artistically and technically the English ballets presented in this season stood comparison with what was being achieved by State-aided national groups anywhere in Europe.

Of the twelve ballets of real distinction—works revealing something more than a slick aptitude for the simpler formulae of experimental choreography—four were by Tudor. Of these, the newest was *Dark Elegies,* created for, and presented in, this season.

In *Dark Elegies* Tudor created a work giving expression to and enriching the significance of the reactions of members of a simple pastoral community to the impact of death. The music used was Mahler's "Kindertotenlieder", and no synopsis, none of the customary stage trappings, were required to convey that this was a highly sensitive and completely unsentimental creation on a theme of death. It is only by assumption (but nothing in the action denies the assumption at any point) that one knows that these peasant figures are enduring the great tragic happening in their lives, the loss of their children. The treatment throughout is remarkable for a refreshing absence of any of the balletic or dramatic clichés of situation, gesture, or dress normally associated with the idea of dying. The Teutonic music (the whole conception of the ballet is a Teutonic rather than a Latin or Celtic idea), together with the Scandinavian inflection of the peasant dresses and the storm-ravaged landscape, confers a tremendous human dignity and power to the slow-stepping ritual dances, adorned by the complex symbolic hand gestures of the mourning congregation. In the individual dances for the different men and women Tudor with great skill and daring has matched the classical neatness of turn and expressiveness of carriage with the freer plastic gestures, drawn from the Central European style of movement. This union of styles is freely leavened with adaptations from steps, gestures, head movements he had watched for in the everyday life of the streets, or amongst dancers in their rehearsal intervals. *Dark Elegies* was the first, and remains the greatest, English work of ballet on a serious theme conceived and executed throughout in a wholly novel technical medium, and with a refreshing freedom from the sometimes embarrassing conventions of what is proper to the depiction of death in the theatre.

By this time one would have thought that Tudor was in an enviable position. He had four good ballets to his credit (an outstanding record for one who had come to ballet comparatively late in life) and as well as dancing for the Ballet Rambert and Sadler's Wells was also working as an arranger of dancing for spectacle plays and television. Surely, if native talent were ever worth the gesture of recognition by what is our equivalent to a National Academy of Dancing, this was the man and now was the time. His unconventional and completely successful merging of the inner rhythms of dance and music in *Descent of Hebe,* the unsentimental pathos of the situation conceived and realised in *Jardin aux Lilas,* the smoothness and daring and languor so subtly drawn from, and expanding into, the music in *The Planets:* all this, crowned by the integrity and moving beauty of *Dark Elegies,* should have brought the recognition which could most fruitfully have benefited him.

By the summer of that year, when the Ballet Rambert toured France with considerable success, Tudor was no longer of the company, nor was he dancing for Sadler's Wells Ballet. With practically no resources, he organised a company of dancers who appeared in a season of his ballets at the Playhouse, Oxford, that July. Financially, the venture was ruinous, but the experience had confirmed in Tudor the ambition to run his own company, presenting his own ballets in the way *he* thought they should be given. Lecturing, producing for television and teaching kept him going whilst his plans for a company of dancers in which there should be neither "stars"—nor too many star-part ballets—matured. That plan came to realisation late in 1938, then only after months of plan-making, plan-breaking, interviewing, rehearsing and conferring, which seemed to have been in vain when the week of the Munich crisis broke over our heads.

The London Ballet formally came into existence in November 1938. Tudor's small company, which had played at the Oxford Playhouse in 1937, had been rehearsing for their first full season throughout six or seven months. Even when the Munich crisis filled everyone with terror and despair, the keynote of conversation amongst the dancers was not the gruesome possibility of air-raids but their concern that "even if war came" the season would take place somehow, somewhere. Many of the dancers were working in films, cabaret, other ballet companies, so that rehearsals were intermittent affairs, mostly exhausting Saturday morning and Sunday all day sessions. Tudor was lecturing on and teaching ballet at evening institutes, appearing in television and with Agnes de Mille at a midsummer season at the Westminster Theatre. Between these and other breadwinning activities, he spent all his waking time either rehearsing or planning some part of the forthcoming season's business.

All the reasons for his breakaway from the Ballet Rambert were not disclosed: there were conflicts of temperament in many directions and much disagreement over the casting and producing of his works: but these were only some of the reasons for his secession from the Ballet Club organisation. Primarily Tudor founded The London Ballet because he believed it the only way to present his ballets as he wished the public to see them. He believed in his achievements and his potentialities. The organisation which could have given him the best background and working conditions was not apparently interested in the work of persons trained and developed outside its orbit.

Toynbee Hall, the first Universities Settlement, had recently rebuilt a part of its premises and now possessed a good theatre of four hundred seats with perfect sight lines, and a well proportioned but somewhat under-lit stage. It was at Toynbee Hall that Tudor lectured and gave lessons to keen amateurs of ballet, and he had found it possible to make terms for the use of this theatre as his headquarters which were within the financial limitations in which he had to operate.

The difficulties to be overcome in bringing the company to birth and presenting it for baptism on a stage before a full auditorium were fantastically many. This was no public theatre which could be hired together with front of house staff, box office, stage crew, electrician, etc., but a private theatre open only to members of an association attached thereto. Before any productions could be planned, an audience had to be found which would guarantee some degree of support for it. And it was a new theatre—brand new—and therefore, as well as building a potential audience, it was necessary to build a complete administration and executive. This personnel for box office, secretarial and clerical work, for lighting, setting, scene shifting, for looking after the front of the house, had to be recruited from willing amateurs. Neither Toynbee Hall nor Antony Tudor could have afforded to pay for the services of the twenty-odd persons necessary. No ballet company faced its last week of rehearsals with so many stones unturned, so many avenues unexplored. The ready money needed for essential working apparatus—scenery, costumes, music parts—and to meet the costs of theatre rent, lighting, pianos, printing, transport, fees for dancers, musicians, arrangers, designers, was all provided by Tudor from his carefully acquired savings.

The complexities were harassing: they were made almost unbearable by frequent bottlenecks in the organisation line. These bottlenecks were due to the top speed at which everything had to be done, and sometimes a process would stop from sheer inertia. Dancers cut meals and tore over to the other side of London between rehearsals in order to fit costumes. Painters worked furiously, silently, on the scene floor and suddenly stopped for lack of materials; then it would be found that no shop within miles could supply what was needed. The focal point towards which all activities converged was the theatre, but no private office or separate telephone existed in the theatre for the exclusive use of the company.

Somehow the last nightmare week ended. Tudor's big following at the evening institutes where he taught and lectured, and the *avant garde* of keen ballet-goers, were all *au fait* with what was developing in ballet. Over cups of tea snatched between rehearsals, dancers and musicians had addressed thousands of circulars. Four days before the opening over 90% of all seats had been booked for the first two performances on 5 and 12 December.

At 8 p.m. on 5 December, 1938, every disengaged dancer in London, most of the musical and theatrical press, the gossip columnists, and what appeared to be about a thousand ardent ballet-goers filled the immaculate plush chairs or stood jammed in a tight phalanx at the back of the stalls. Contrary to the naïve expectations of certain parts of the audience there were few tail coats and backless gowns—and even fewer silk chokers and hobnailed boots. Ballet had come to the East End, not as an act of patronage to the East Enders, but for good practical reasons. A good theatre existed in the heart of the East End, a large part of the ballet-going public lived in or near the district, and the West End commercial theatres were out of reach on account of their excessive operational costs.

The opening programme consisted of *Gala Performance,* a new ballet about ballet, to Prokofiev music; the established favourite, *Jardin aux Lilas* (which I believe Tudor then thought the best drawing card; it was always his own preference among his works), *Judgment of Paris* and *Gallant Assembly.* The dancers were nervous but controlled for the first few minutes; after the first change of scene confidence plus the enthusiasm of the audience served to cut the final bonds of tension which had gripped them and they danced with fire and ice in their veins. Backstage was seething with scene-shifters, assistant electricians, amateur dressers, friends. Disconsolate followers of the dancers, who had got hopelessly lost on the way, kept on arriving almost up to the final curtain. There was no room anywhere in the theatre and they waited in a huddled knot peering through a small window in one of the wing doors which gave a view across part of the backcloth, on which now and then a leg in arabesque or a detached arm would be visible.

Long after the last curtain, everyone stayed on discussing the performance, all dazed by the fact that such professional—in the best sense of the word—results had been achieved in this so unprofessional theatre. Hugh Stevenson's rococo costumes for *Gala Performance* with the regal opulence of the setting backed by the gay pink and white fountains was the most lavish décor he had yet achieved. *Jardin aux Lilas,* the embarrassing moral fable *Judgment of Paris,* owing nothing to mythology but its title, and the raffish, cynical *Gallant Assembly* made up a sufficiently varied programme. There were not—and would not be for some years—any "classical" ballets. Tudor was convinced that the best sort of classical dancing could be set inside modern ballets. He was essentially a "dancer's choreographer": he cared more for the lyric or tragic or comic atmosphere, and its creation by a meticulous observance of the movement sequence, than about any other factor in his ballets. Or, to put it another way, he cared so much for pure dancing that he gave the major part of his imagination as a choreographer to the bar-by-bar phrasing of every part of every dance. The texture of every part of each movement he devised was elaborated with care. I think this preoccupation, whilst it helped to create some of the most *refined* dancing in modern ballet, left little time for other choreographic detail. The rare, but noticeable, weaknesses in plot, the flaws in musicality here and there, and the psychological falseness of character found now and then in his works are perhaps only temporary faults. They are some of the minor obstacles on the way to the higher ranks of choreography which can be overcome perhaps by closer co-operation with musicians, designers and authors in the planning of his future big ballets.

Of the works presented during that winter by the London Ballet, four had been in existence for some time—*The Planets, Descent of Hebe, Jardin aux Lilas* and *Dark Elegies. Gala Performance* and *Soirée musicale* had been created for this season, and *Gallant Assembly* had been the new ballet for the Oxford venture in 1937. *Judgment of Paris* was composed in 1938 and first presented in the Agnes de Mille season at the Westminster Theatre. Together with a divertissement, the addition to *The Planets,* and that choreographic gem, *The Shepherd's Wooing* (an excerpt from Balanchine's *Gods Go a-Begging,* 1928) there were sufficient works to present balanced programmes of the established and the newer Tudor signatures throughout the series of fortnightly performances.

The complications gradually lessened, but there was no performance unmarked by some incident, gay or grave, or some sudden contretemps which invariably declined into a mere temporary derangement of either the Director's or the Manager's nervous system. Two further ballets were in preparation for the latter part of the season, but the inevitable balletic complication (lack of funds) delayed further and further the purchase of settings and costumes. Tudor had no illusions, from the very beginning of the season, about the possible financial returns from the sale of seats. If the whole house had sold out for every performance there would scarcely have been sufficient balance over running expenses to put on the two new works, let alone provide the sum required for the more ambitious plans of the following winter.

Tudor was in the same position as every other producer-impresario lacking extensive backing. Seasons are always started on "just enough" money; which always means just not quite enough owing to the mysterious way in which all theatrical finances require floating sums to meet accounts whose length can never accurately be forecast. For it is of the absolute essence of theatre that the advance plans of a repertorial group will have to be adjusted at the end of the first month. Either the venture is stabilised at a hairsbreadth from insolvency (assuming it has not failed) or the opening month has brought such success that new works have to be hurried forward and old ones remounted or re-dressed for possible tours and return seasons. Buoyed by the examination of account books with a favourable balance, the directorate accepts offers of touring engagements (possibly on graduated percentages of the box office takings) and plans "return seasons" in London. This automatically brings forward the presentation of next summer's new works to this autumn, and the extraction from cold-store of last year's or the year before's achievements; they always need new trimmings of some sort and the production requires either hotting-up or cooling-off, all of which costs money. Theatrical fortune is so fickle that impresarios of repertory material have to be alert to every chance of keeping a company going once it is founded. The booking agents' business of providing the provincial theatres with fifty-two different "attractions" a year is full of complexities. Whole areas, or whole categories of town, are uncertain ground for such special lines as Shakespearian repertory, opera, ballet, or, in fact, anything more complicated than "The Adventures of Alphonse the Apache" or "His Jungle Bride". What succeeds in Plymouth may be anathema to Pontefract, and something that "had 'em standing on the seats and yelling" in London may be the spectacle from which they stay away in thousands all over the provinces.

Tudor's hope was the hope of everybody, from Diaghilev down, who ever ran a ballet company, and that was, that somebody, preferably with both money and taste, would see the company's ballets and be pleased to give patronage to a venture so obviously worthy of continuance.

Antony Tudor had less than the usual amount of good fortune in this respect. Various ladies and gentlemen interested in ballet came, saw, offered congratulations, and went their ways. When the season closed at the end of April, 1939, the company was intact, it had several television dates to fulfil, and Tudor had earned for it and for himself the privilege of creating and dancing the ballet sections of such operas-with-ballet as were to be presented in the Covent Garden summer season. By then, how much had been achieved for the good of ballet? what prospects had the hard-working dancers and musicians? what hopes had Tudor of seeing in concrete form the larger-scale ballets he was planning for the future?

The performances by Tudor's own company of *Dark Elegies* and *Jardin aux Lilas,* always presented with delicacy and restraint, had established these ballets as, respectively, the best serious-subject English ballet, and one of the best-balanced short lyric ballets in any repertoire. The concert hall impression of Chausson's "Poème" is maudlin, but heard in the theatre whilst we watch the despairing manoeuvring of the lovers, about to be parted for ever, in the moonlit garden after the wedding feast, it forms part of a pathetic symphony of music and movement.

*Gala Performance* had a magnificent setting, superb dresses, bitter-sweet music and much ingenuity and solemnly pure 'classical' dancing, but lacked clarity of effect. As C. W. Beaumont pointed out in the best review written yet on this ballet (*International Post,* 6 April, 1939): "If the intention is to present a period pastiche there must be some attempt to match music, choreography and setting. Delibes, Widor or Messager, for instance, would fit; but Prokofiev, one of the most modernist of composers, seems out of the picture." The transition from the Backstage scene into the Performance proper is always something of a shock, but the shock fades quickly before the outrageous charm of the ballerina from Moscow, the smart pomposity of the cavaliers and the cool refinement of both breeding and dancing seen in the Milanese ballerina. At its best, this ballet is a series of vignette-caricatures of dancers being cynical, charming, uproariously funny and ironically dignified, but it does lack any sort of thread holding together beginning, middle and end. Prokofiev's "Classical Symphony" seems to me exactly right as background to an ironic study of ballet-from-the-inside, but not (as Mr Beaumont suggests) ballet of this particular genre.

The other Tudor works outside his Ballet Rambert days were *Soirée Musicale, Gallant Assembly, Judgment of Paris* and the added episode "Mercury" in *The Planets.* The first of these was created just before the opening of the Toynbee Hall season, and is based on a suite of Rossini pieces orchestrated by Britten; the six dances are a pretty assembly of ballet-cum-national idioms in costumes suggested by early 19th century prints, yet unimpeded by the voluminousness and weight of that period's dress. The Bolero is by far the finest balletisation of this particular form, born out of and, in return, supporting, the music. Tudor never saw the superb backcloth which, later, Hugh Stevenson designed and which, with the gold-and-pink settees, gave to the dances just that little extra suggestion of serio-comic baroque implicit in the music and costumes.

*Gallant Assembly,* a seventeenth-century interlude, had charming music of Tartini, heroic and extremely danceable costumes and a stately bronze-green and black setting, again by Stevenson. In a mock pastoral episode the salacious scamperings of a group of 'aristocrats in love' are interrupted by the gentle *pas-de-deux* of a pair of 'hired performers' revealed when a magnificent palanquin is borne into the presence of hosts and guests. Fascinated by the simplicity and youth of the young couple, the aristocrats attempt forthwith to seduce them both, receiving for all their pains only dignified rebuffs which prelude the rapid break-up of the festivities. The outburst of vituperation against Tudor for the creation of *Judgment of Paris* could better have been directed against *Gallant Assembly,* whose initial performance a female spectator summed up succinctly in: "Gallant Assembly? It ought to be called just Dirty Party!"

*Judgment of Paris* is not, I think, the remorseless piece of documentary on prostitution that some have assessed it as. The 'Judgment' is that of a trio of café ladies on the drunken idiot who finishes his Parisian night's entertainment in their company. After summoning each one to dance before him, he drinks deeper and deeper, thus signifying to the ladies that all their enticements have been in vain. He collapses into a drunken stupor and the three goddesses, irate at his failure to come to terms with any one of them, surround his soggy carcase and strip him of pocket book, purse, loose change and gold watch and chain. The ballet is not lacking in effectiveness because it is based on recognition of the fact that the female habituées of this sort of café in the Paris of the nineties are unlikely to be earning their livelihood as seamstresses or housemaids. A whole period of French painting is summed in the genre of impressions of the raffish night life, centred in deep drinking, heavy gambling and unlimited prostitution. Any aspect of living anywhere under the sun is a plausible starting point for a choreographer as much as for a poet, painter or dramatist.

When Tudor added "Mercury" to *The Planets* he created two of his most difficult dancing parts in the characters of The Planet and The Mortal born under its influence. Their patterns, a broken counterpoint to the music, reproduce exactly in the movement medium the brittle yet luscious qualities of Light and Liquidity which are the music's reflection of both the mythical Mercury and the exciting volatility of quicksilver.

Not one of these ballets is in any essential a dated production: either by unsuitable topicality, unfashionableness as a vogue piece or in its lack of coherence as a trial work. This is the respect in which Tudor's achievements are remarkable in English ballet. When he may have created, perhaps, twenty other works, not only *Dark Elegies* and *Jardin aux Lilas,* but also *Descent of Hebe, Gala Performance* and *Judgment of Paris* will bear revival. The secret of this sort of success lies, of course, in the texture of the dancing. It is whole cloth, well woven from strong strands, cleverly cut and skilfully tailored: like those dignified garments one still sees in remote rural places adorning some patriarchal shepherd on a Sabbath, they will outlast last year's and this year's fashionably bright, but essentially shoddy garments which mass-production so remorselessly provides for the mass appetite.

The outbreak of war cut the ground away from under everyone's feet in the theatre. After the first dark weeks of closed houses, only those with resources and profitable commitments were able to get into stride again, either in London or on the road. Plans for the London Ballet's winter campaign had been drawn up by Tudor, and few people shared his knowledge of where, when and on what terms the next performance was to be given. Between the beginning and the end of September, most of those exercising any degree of control over their circumstances and employment had embarked on plans which radically altered the course of the next two years' activities. Tudor had been invited, early in the year, to visit New York as guest-choreographer, representative of the art of ballet in this country. The invitation was pressed again, and believing absolutely, by mid-September, that nothing could be arranged to guarantee the London Ballet's survival through that winter, he sailed for America early in October. He made the voyage in company with Andrée Howard, the other guest choreographer of the Ballet Theatre.

It was some time after Tudor's departure that Harold Rubin, the new proprietor-manager of the Arts Theatre Club, revealed himself as the mystery man with whom Tudor had been negotiating that summer. The plan had apparently been for Tudor to provide a ballet company to perform in the Arts Theatre (to help build up the Club as a ballet centre) in return for almost complete freedom from financial responsibility. The summer conferences between this prospective impresario and Antony Tudor seem to have consisted of endless interviews during which detailed analyses and forecasts were made respecting every sixpence of the London Ballet's past, present and future budgets. All this, for reasons known to himself only at that time, Tudor had kept secret from those who had built up the Company with him, and whose immediate future in ballet was linked with a possibly successful winter season in 1939/40.

The story, when told, of how Peggy van Praagh, with the co-operation of nearly every original member of the Company, succeeded under truly appalling difficulties in organising and directing the Company through 1939, 1940 and 1941, will present a picture of some of the funniest and some of the more grim moments endured in war-time ballet in this country.

Tudor's career from October 1939 onwards, will be, inescapably, an American career. Now (January 1942) there is less chance than ever of his returning to direct, dance or make ballets here while war continues. All the circumstances that made the colourful history of English ballet between 1930 and 1939 conspired to give him just one big chance—the founding of the London Ballet on an ideal not unworthy of the greatest figures in ballet history. Circumstances altered suddenly the balance of external events, and Antony Tudor's London Ballet became the London Ballet trying to carry out Tudor's policy, but without his presence, and therefore lacking the drive of his creative imagination. What he does now across the Atlantic is of a fresh type, of other proportions, and bearing an altogether different personal inflection from the works he created here.

## DARK ELEGIES
From *A Prejudice for Ballet*.
Ballet by Antony Tudor. Music by Mahler. Dress and Décor by Nadia Benois.

For almost twenty years people have been watching *Les Sylphides,* approving its ideology, accepting its simple and fascinating enactments with the material of classicism, and accepting the presentation of one of the major works of ballet without being greatly disturbed by its lack of story content. When, many years after the composition of *Les Sylphides,* Massine scored a full-length work using an extension of the same material and created a work capable of arousing and sustaining interest without story content, very few people found themselves able to accept this fresh orientation of ideology and terminology. But very gradually it is being realised that *Choreartium* was no stunt over the grave of the dead Brahms; it marked a turning-point logically reached on the road of balletic progression first signposted by Fokine. One of the first indices of an awareness of the existence of this path (amongst choreographers) was the creation of *Dark Elegies* by a comparatively young English dancer-choreographer, Antony Tudor, during the winter of 1936. Apart from some of the abstract patternings of Leonide Massine the corpus of works of the Rambert Ballet represents the only sustained attempt for a long while to get ballet away from the old channels; limited by a miniature stage, a small body of dancers and a lack of orchestral accompaniment, the composers of ballet at the Ballet Club have exploited every variant of the older idioms of choreography, staging, mime-pattern, and movement to create works in a fresher idiom than the more commercially restricted units use. A series of interesting choreographic experiments with all the usual material of ballet was crowned in the composition of *Dark Elegies*.

The music is an adaptation of Mahler's *Kindertotenlieder*, a song-cycle whose literal title ('Songs for the deaths of children') is implied but condensed into the two-word title of the ballet; the orchestral accompaniment for the cycle is the score used for the ballet, and it comments with restraint—yet with the intensity which informs all solemn music scored without the obvious tricks of evocation of sorrow—on the eternal release from, and solution of, living in death. Here is most definitely a case of the music being expanded in its purpose, as it were, by the supporting visual imagery enacted. The melodic range is minuscular combined with vast subtleties of harmonic usage and rhythms of the utmost delicacy, very skilfully used. The dance scoring effects its parallels with the music with the same integrity and lack of what must be called 'ballet theatricality' as do *Les Sylphides* and the major Massine work *Choreartium*. There is no story to illustrate, no moral to point, no philosophy to expound; the combined structure of music and movement expends itself in an outburst of grief and despair, the exposition of the reaction towards some kind of hope, a resurrection of faith and, finally, the evocation of the renewed trust in, and love for, those still left to us after the visitation of death.

Four male soloists, three females, and a female chorus effect the whole sequence of images in a range of motion and stasis forms whose apparent simplicity belies the rigorous grounding in classicism which has made them possible, and at the same time amply demonstrates the elasticity of the technique based on the five positions. There is only a very limited use of point and half-point, nothing of even the simplest form of adagio acrobatics, but a delicate and complex range of arm and hand movements and poses of the head such as ballet has rarely before attempted. Tudor has shown particular regard for the most subtle instrument that a choreographer can use—stasis. In the hands of a choreographer of genius, stasis is as effective as its musical counterpart, silence, is in the hands of a great composer; and Antony Tudor's use of it in this work is as aesthetically sure as was Massine's balanced composing of the magnificent groupings in the first movement of *Choreartium*.

The décor of Nadia Benois achieves almost absolute perfection; the condition which, for the writer, bars it from the highest pinnacle is the fact of its obvious stressing of a Scandinavian or Finnish landscape in the icy blue of the great lake, the wind-tortured trees in the foreground, the great berg-like rocks rearing their heads above the lake's surface, and the northern mountains behind the pine forest. The similarity of ranges of evocation, one suggests, to the non-Latin European mind, of both Mahler's and Sibelius's music, is very close. Parts of the First and Second Symphonies and the *Kalevala* suggest imagery of suffering, despair, and majestic resignation closely parallel to the imagery of the Mahler score; and it is an awareness of this parallelism that accents the reference (possibly, by the designer, an unconsciously achieved one) between Mahler and the Finnish composer, in the backcloth of steel-bright water, rocks and pines. Attention to the smooth fusion of movement and music was from time to time intruded upon by the memory of Sibelius's work and the inescapable comparisons suggested thereby.

### POSTSCRIPT ON TUDOR

Coton's views on Tudor would be incomplete without mention of some later works. He wrote from New York in *The Daily Telegraph* on 29 March, 1966.

Under the artistic direction of Dame Alicia Markova the Ballet of the Metropolitan Opera House last night presented three ballets seen for the first time in the United States. The evening was largely a triumph for the English choreographer Antony Tudor. His new work, *Concerning Oracles,* shows the faults of a choreographer too long absent from regular ballet-making. Situations are slow in development and secondary characters too imprecise. Yet, simultaneously, it reveals Tudor's unique capacity to create human-sized characters through classical dance movement undistorted by naturalism.

Each of the three episodes, Elizabethan, Romantic Period and Maupassant Pastoral, centres on people's reactions to the impact of prophecies. The triple action is linked by a fortune teller dispensing spells, gruesome symbols and Tarot cards.

The first two incidents carry overtones of wonder and horror while the third explodes into the furiously comic yet unhappy adventures of a gauche youth seeking the admiration of a lovely woman.

Despite the neatness of the score, compounded of three orchestral miniatures by Jacques Ibert, and the aptness of the scenario as a dance-drama, the three episodes do not create a bold triptych commemorating the behaviour of victims of supernatural possession. Tudor's alchemy fails in its total effect because this group of technically able dancers are, on the whole, insufficiently sophisticated to give real depth to his sardonically imagined characters.

By contrast, *Echoing of Trumpets,* originally produced in Stockholm in 1963, made its searing comment on man's inhumanity to man with greatest effect. Of no special time and place, this is a parable about the oppressed and the oppressors.

To a suite by Bohuslav Martinu, it shows the events of one day in an occupied village where the still-resisting victims defy their military conquerors. This is a Tudor masterpiece with every step, gesture and grouping used to dynamic effect in depicting violence, courage and self-sacrifice.

Where the first ballet failed to expound completely its tenuous fable through subtle dance-imagery, *Echoing of Trumpets* emerged as an epic statement on human behaviour whose every situation was loaded with truth and compassion.

From *The Daily Telegraph*, 26 January, 1967.
Originality of theme allied with inventive dance-imagery can produce a ballet which may be either a despair or a delight; it rather depends on what you expect dancing to "tell" you. Antony Tudor staged *Shadowplay* last night at Covent Garden, a ballet about nothing that was obvious and about almost everything that is usually thought non-balletic.

A young boy living in some jungle has a series of encounters with creatures of the trees, the air, the earth and, finally, the heavens. So that none of these creatures can be labelled absolutely as "man", "ape", or "god," all of them have vestigial tails—possibly representing the four significant levels of the ape world? The boy assumes a certain authority over some of the creatures, accepts others as no different from himself, is wonder-struck but not overwhelmed by the celestial beings.

No lesson is offered, no wrapped-up conclusion is provided: we are watching, perhaps, a human struggling to understand certain shadowy beings present only in his imagination. This is truly a shadow play, with its part amusing, part solemn encounters and entanglements taking place in that vague region that belongs neither to darkness nor to light.

The whole work is twenty-five minutes' worth of dancing, dance acting and a creation of delicate atmospheres and its most telling effect was that it seemed to spread its narration over a few seconds and, simultaneously, a handful of centuries.

The Charles Koechlin music consists of excerpts from works partly inspired by Kipling's Indian tales, but the ballet affords little comparison with Kipling's characters or their values. A finely-drilled cast, headed by Anthony Dowell (the Boy), Merle Park (a celestial) and Derek Rencher (a terrestrial) danced with a suitable precision and vivacity required by the choreography. Mr Dowell, with limited characterising experience so far, contrived to bring out very effectively the boy's wonder, anxiety, resentment and enmity inspired by the shadowy figments of his imagination—or were they primeval powers returning to this jungle thousands of years after their original creation?

From *The Daily Telegraph*, 26 November, 1968.
A creation by a master choreographer which fails to reach perfection can yet fascinate by the vivacity or originality of its several parts, the theme, music, décor, or dance style.

Many such fascinations were revealed in *Knight Errant*, a new ballet by Antony Tudor presented last night at the Opera House, Manchester, by the Royal Ballet Touring Section. But the ballet is overlong in development, imprecise in dramatic structure and often weak in its choreographic design. Yoked rigidly to a number of extracts from several works of Richard Strauss, the story is derived from that suddenly popular French novel, *Les Liaisons Dangereuses*.

In a delicately stylised 18th century setting by Stefanos Lazaridis, it depicts the activities of the title character, Chevalier d'Amour, during a complex series of adventures which include three separate seductions. The three victims are each identically white-clad and there is some occasional witty misunderstanding between the Chevalier and the lady of that particular moment—who may or may not be the partner in the previous or the subsequent adventure.

But this is optimistically to read as much as one dare into a ballet which aesthetically ranges too widely between the exquisite and the banal, with many occasional pauses in between for glimpses of the obvious.

From such a skilled creator, the most puzzling aspect of this ballet is the unwieldy manner of introducing characters and developing the story. Tudor deploys various ensembles to provide frameworks for the principals, using mostly an unimaginative vocabulary of steps emulating 18th century social dancing. There is very imprecise use of the lackeys who enact a species of living furniture to frame the seductions; and of the Chevalier's attendant lady, who is not made sufficiently positive to mean much to the action.

This is basically a witty scenario but largely foiled in the telling by much dull choreography and an obvious overweight of music.

## (iii) FREDERICK ASHTON

Coton's appreciations of Ashton reproduced here have been collected from many shorter notices from a variety of sources. The account of *Les Patineurs*, created in 1937, is taken from *A Prejudice for Ballet*.

### LES PATINEURS

Choreography by Ashton. Music by Meyerbeer. Décor and Dress by William Chappell.

In this work Ashton escaped, for a while at least, the convention of the necessity of scoring ballet to story; a convention which ominously threatens to stifle all inventiveness in choreographers to-day. As with his earlier *Capriol Suite* and *Façade,* the terminology for the dance was provided by the period and occasion depicted. The setting is of an ice rink and, so far as any locale is indicated, it may be in the Vienna or other equally modish city of gaiety of the period. The dress notation suggests also the Teutonic; hefty young gallants and rosy-cheeked maidens will be the executants of the skating patterns. A few trellis arches form the background and wings, and deeper still, a cloth of a few wind-swept and bare trees against a night-blue sky completes the suggestion of a midwinter carnival occasion; small paper lanterns hang from the trellis. To the simple measures of the tuneful yet undistracting music, the skaters make their entry: the two blue-clad Ice Maidens trip pertly across in bunched skirts and ribboned hats, decorated with frills and ruchings; they carry little muffs; and as they set the pattern in a note of gaiety, confidently and archly glowing to the audience, they complete their track and exit: they are instantly followed by the eight-part mixed chorus, clad in russet and blue, which glides in to etch its patterns on the smooth ice.

The whole of the dancing is conditioned by the temporary convention that everyone is moving on ice, and every step and stance is rigidly controlled in the peculiarly stiff-thighed and straight-backed walk of the ice-skater. After the series of neat traverses and diagonal figurings, the chorus links in pairs, circles once the round of the stage, then glides off in the slowly accelerating, rippling rhythm of the skater building up speed; the variation is danced by a tight and wiry figure in navy and sky blue, trimmed with white fur, a bright and apt costume which is, incidentally, one of the best-designed costumes anywhere in ballet. Here a superb and dashing skater is demonstrating his skill, defying all laws of equilibrium in every movement and pose, accenting his skill by a succession of jumps culminating in flat falls to earth, skilfully ending in three-point contacts with the stage; the flooring cracks audibly at each hard blow, as, simultaneously, hand and knee meet stage together. A *pas-de-deux* for a pair of lyric figures follows this brilliant character exercise; a deliberately romantic incursion into the unsophisticate fun, danced by a male in tight-fitting satin and fur, with a female partner in gauzy satin and muslin, fur-trimmed.

The nostalgic music affords a variation in terms of a too rapid adagio patterning, and in the music's accidental reference to a Tchaikovskian theme the action is jarred by the inevitable evocation of a passage in *Lac des Cygnes*. One is almost persuaded that the choreographer has unconsciously aped the pattern of the older work. At the next change of rhythm, the chorus returns with the blue-clad pair, and two new females are introduced, decked in maroon and white. The lyric figure is broken and the full assembly sketches a spirited jig and galop, broken to allow swift demonstrations by the duos of soubrettes, the heroic variation figure, and the white-clad pair, who have been drawn into the general grouping. So the pattern is woven with a growing succession of neater and more daring spins, *pirouettes,* moving arabesque figures and series of elaborately furious turns; the variation figure leads in the blue-clad twins and each vies with the other in a breathless and extensive fury of single and double *fouettés,* close turns, and widely flung *jetés.* The variation figure links all the subsequent demonstration pieces with a succession of brief interludes of transverse flight, each time creating a fresh variation in his idiom of moving arabesques and seemingly limitless *pirouettes.* The pace of the dancing rises with the music's tempo as the gaily shrill melodies draw the dancers across, down, and up-stage in solo, in duo, and in supported groupings making more and more daring experiments with equilibrium as the hot pace rises.

The massed stage floods neatly into a complexly mathematical range of design, whose patterns cease or elide as quickly as they are formed. Every figure, male and female, drives the last possible phase of ingenuity and speed into the whirling maze. Two by two the pairs create their final designs on the glittering surface, mark their last signatures of mode, and, as the lights dim and the soft snowflakes eddy in mid-stage, the blue-clad leader of the rout leaps in, spins high, and crashes into the centre-stage; in a series of jumps as though testing the surface for strain he bounces, then, as the music gaily rattles into the coda, with brass thundering and choking in full clamour, he sets a series of spins on one foot: with free leg extended horizontally stiff and arms driving the helical patterning remorselessly into a higher and madder speed. We count ten, twelve, sixteen turns as the acceleration grows and the strings rocket the peroration up-scale: the brass roars shudderingly as the exciting finale tears towards the last bars: the curtain is slowly closing and the eddying flakes whirl around the thrilling speedy device as the figure is hidden. As the last brazen glory is wound out, the curtain swiftly rushes up, the lights dim even lower and we see the effortless endless series of turns winding smoothly on . . . and on . . .and on . . . The curtain snaps shut at the final bar, leaving the dancer in mid-flight spinning until the last ounce of momentum that he can create finally breaks the figure. The effectiveness of this daring and simple curtain is superb ballet, superb stagecraft, and dramatic, of its own intensity, in a way that balletic sequences rarely achieve; it is the very utmost note of éclat needed to dress this demonstration of the transition of one code of athletic movement into the rarefying and noble patterns of dancing.

## DAPHNIS AND CHLOE
From *Public Opinion*, 13 April, 1951.

Fokine began this century's ballet reformation—the movement which has given all vitality to this art in our time—with the novel suggestions for ballet production which were attached to his original scenario for *Daphnis and Chloë*. This was offered to his director at St Petersburg in 1904, and was disregarded; in 1912 Fokine created the ballet, but under difficulties which led him to resign from the Diaghilev Company. He produced the work later in America, and yet another version was created in America for the Philadelphia Ballet by Catherine Littlefield. To the same music of Ravel and the identical scenario, Frederick Ashton last week created his 1951 ballet for Covent Garden. Fokine's prototype is important because in it he showed the fullest possible realisation of the hypothesis from which the art of ballet has drawn its greatest strength during this century's renaissance—that a fresh dance-style to match the subject must be invented for each new ballet and, further, that it is desirable to use freshly written music as well as freshly designed costumes and sets.

Mr Ashton has followed faithfully the story derived from Longus and has received full collaboration from his designer, John Craxton; the Ravel music was given completely, using the chorus which was not always present in previous productions. The success of this version depends on the degree of invention of movement shown by the choreographer; there are interesting solos for Chloë, Daphnis, and Dorkon, the rival of Daphnis; there are well-conceived ensemble dances for the Shepherds and Shepherdesses and for the Pirates; of these the outstanding creation is the solo dance of Chloë (Margot Fonteyn) when she is captured by the pirates. The remainder of the ballet is mostly made up of dance and mimic action reminiscent of much of the choreographer's earlier work. The music imposes on rather than supports the choreographer, for it so nearly completely says everything that can be uttered about the situations that it demands a very economical movement-style—a kind of visual overtone to the music—to accompany it. Such movement, throughout the ballet, must show the same continuous organic growth as the music reveals. In the present version the mingling of Greek, Cretan and what appear to be Balkan folk-dance elements (for the choruses of Shepherds and Pirates) is contrasted startlingly with the academic classical style given to the female dancers; the use of the *pointe* in all the important dances for females makes an incongruous contrast with the vigorous peasant-type steps shown by the male dancers. The ingenuities are many, and with the material offered to them each of the soloists gives an interesting version of the character portrayed, but, in general, the dancing falls into episodes rather than into a continuously woven pattern complementing the subtle pattern of the music.

Mr Craxton's constructions, backcloths and costumes do not blend happily together; the scenery does not compose into a unique stylisation of tones and shapes, and beside it the costumes are mostly realistic copies of contemporary dress. The intention may well have been to create a contemporary visualisation of the story, in which case the dance-patterns should surely have been created as a complete theatrical stylising of modern Hellenic folk and social dancing. The work is a highly sincere effort and the performers gave everything possible to their rôles; particular praise go to Margot Fonteyn and John Field (Dorkon) for full realisation—within the style of movement—of the characters they essayed.

## SCENES DE BALLET
From *Ballet Today*, May, 1956.

Although *Scènes de Ballet* had been given quite frequently on the American tour, it has not been seen here for a long while. It was a welcome addition to a repertory which leans heavily on classics and elaborate story-ballets: it remains, I am convinced, one of Ashton's best-ever efforts in the *genre* of abstract dance pictorialism.

Few modern ballet-goers will have experienced the first big work in this style, when Massine, in 1928, created *Ode*—a phenomenally beautiful ballet which got right away from the two existing major categories—the classical "white" ballet and the short one-acter of intense dramatic or comic type. Massine broke new ground in framing an allegorical tale in completely new kinds of groupings, fresh, acrobatic-style dances, solemn, but moving processionals: all this set in amazingly new kinds of costume and with daring new methods of stylised staging, décor and inventive lighting. The idea was carried to its fullest possibility five years later in *Choreartium*. At the same time and from a completely different point of approach, Balanchine was working out ballets, using nothing but the purest classical vocabulary, in which no story happened, but our imaginations were stirred, our sense of pictorial beauty stimulated, by the manipulation of disciplined bodies in disciplined patterns of dancing.

*Scènes de Ballet* is, in one sense, as complete a ballet as are, for instance, *Les Sylphides* or Balanchine's *Apollo*. It compares with *Giselle* in the same way that, musically, a Mozart quartet compares with a symphony by Schumann: one appeals *first* to our aesthetic sensitiveness, the other to our dramatic instinct. Each is legitimate ballet, each has a different kind of satisfaction to offer us.

In the revival, David Blair gave brilliant performances in the leading male role and the male quartet—whose choreography is as excitingly novel as was the best male chorus work in *Choreartium*—danced as these parts were never danced before.

## ONDINE
From *The Spectator*, 31 October, 1958.

Fifty years from now theatre historians will hold decided views about our preoccupation, in the 1950s and 1960s, with reviving the three-act ballet convention. To them it will be apparent either that it was wasteful of effort and imagination to try to resurrect the idea of the Romantic Period ballet a hundred years later: or that the three-acter *is* the legitimate mode of expression for a theatrically meaningful dance drama. The ascendancy that the one-acter enjoyed from 1910 on may seem to them an interesting aberration explicable only by the fickleness of managerial policy or the laziness of choreographers.

Covent Garden's production this week of *Ondine* provides no evidence to favour either side of this prospective argument. It has some of the advantages—and the shortcomings, too—of the big-scale Romantic ballet of the nineteenth century. Its revelation of the complexity of artistic and technical problems involved reaffirms for us the skill of those nineteenth-century masters who created the few ballets that have lasted for more than a generation. Further, it underlines our suspicion that nine out of ten of the 400-odd large-scale ballets staged in Europe last century were pretty inept concoctions. Trim away the swooning tributes to certain ballerinas, and the rest of the printed record (even including score, synopsis, designs) indicates that they failed to survive for the excellent reason that there was nothing worth saving.

Choreography is the catalyst working on the ingredients of a ballet which enables them to merge and blend and sustain each other; good music, staging, *décor,* costume, even when supported by quality dancers, amount to nothing unless a choreographic imagination is controlling the actions and interactions between story, dance-image, mime, musical phrase and all the pictorial elements. Frederick Ashton displays again, as in *Cinderella* and his Danish *Romeo and Juliet,* that he can invent and adapt and paraphrase and generally turn inside-out-and-back-again any notion of stylised movement that is usable on today's ballet stage. *Ondine* is the biggest challenge he has yet met. Either he could fashion its components into a contemporary assessment of the mortal-*v*-supernatural struggle depicted or he could choose (as he seems to have done) to attempt a re-creation of the Ondine legend as it occurred in ballets by Perrot and the two Taglionis a hundred years ago.

The result is a story almost identical with those of the old ballets, narrated in Ashton's modern adaptation of classical ballet style. We have to take for granted the subsidiary characters—all the humans. Only Ondine is given a unique personality. The Prince-hero, his betrothed, the Hermit, sailors, attendants, lords and ladies, etc., in dress, manner and movement idiom are so much conventional decoration to a story which concentrates on the mysterious character of Ondine herself.

It is, in fact, pure fairy tale, and if today we can feel that one of ballet's purposes is to present, with modest refurbishings, the more successful of the Romantic Era's fairy tales, *Ondine* has made a place for itself in our repertoire. It gains its effectiveness largely from the supernormal sensitivity of feeling, interaction and mutual understanding which exists between Ashton and his heroine: precisely where some startling or beautiful phase of motion or gesture arises from the choreographer's mind or from Margot Fonteyn's sensibility is impossible to decide. Between them they bring to convincing life—whether earthy, aerial or submarine in quality—a pathetically beautiful character. Her domination over three acts effortlessly overwhelms the more blatant shortcomings of a thin score, some indifferent *décor* and, in certain passages, ensemble dances graced neither by originality nor clarity of presentation. But this production marks no new trend, establishes no fresh convention for twentieth-century ballet, nor indicates a farther frontier towards which we must explore. At this moment, it shows that English ballet is marking time, not stepping off positively into any new direction.

## LA FILLE MAL GARDEE
From *The Daily Telegraph*, 29 January, 1960.

It is debatable whether the existence of the ballet *La Fille mal gardée* for nearly two centuries has rested on its being the first realistic bucolic comedy or because it provides a three-dimensional and amply detailed rôle for a fine dancer-comedienne. The production of Ashton's new version by the Royal Ballet at Covent Garden last night does not settle this point. For this version succeeds partly as naturalistic comedy, partly through its leading dancers' interpretations.

The story is as old as the hills and almost as foolproof. Boy meets Girl—Boy and Girl are parted—Opposition defeated by a trick—Boy gets Girl.

The principal roles are a strenuous test which Nadia Nerina as Lise and David Blair as Colas meet with ease. Miss Nerina deploys all her customary fluency in dances which Ashton has carefully tailored to her talent; her acting of the subtle changes of situation that continually involve her was, at points, variable.

David Blair danced with splendid assurance, even in the testing virtuosities specially created for the rôle. His acting tended to be in a single key; he was a charming gallant youth, perhaps too elegant in manner for these rustic scenes and events.

The third big rôle is that of Widow Simone, Lise's mother, always a male interpretation. This characterisation, for real effect, is as difficult a task as that of the ballerina, and Stanley Holden brings to it the craft and experience of many years of character-playing. He is costumed and made up to resemble Nellie Wallace and a lot of his "business' is very like that of a pantomime dame.

All the rôles are developed through comedy of circumstance—not comedy of character. The choreography has been so arranged that it depends, as in no other ballet I know, on objects, tricks and apparatus. There are dances with sickles, with bottles, with cornsheafs, and a whole compendium of ribbon dances. Significant use is made of an umbrella, a maypole, a churn and even a real pony (eating real sugar, too!) on stage.

All this apparatus tends to hinder the smooth running of the plot through what should seem inevitable and continuous phases of dancing and acting. But altogether the ballet succeeds as a lightweight entertainment, with much charm, some fine comedy, some more dubious.

Alexander Grant as the stupid suitor whom Lise easily circumvents danced and acted in a suitably eccentric mode with enormous effect.

The period music of Hérold (1828) runs smoothly enough. Osbert Lancaster's décor and costumes are solidly effective rather than creating that diverting enchantment expected.

## (iv) MARKOVA AND FONTEYN

### 'BALLERINA': A DEFINITION

Excerpts from article 'On a Future Ballerina', *Ballet*, October, 1946.

Perhaps it would be best to start with a definition. At least six centuries ago the word *ballerina* was in use in Italy and meant simply a female dancer. By the time that professional dancers emerged in French ballet the title applied to an outstanding professional female dancer. The Romantic ballet of the early nineteenth century was marked by a quite new concept of feminine dancing, and from this era the definition strictly applies to an outstanding female soloist dancer ranking as a principal in a company of dancers. It retained this meaning right through to the Diaghilev era; after all, it has been a title applicable at varying times to such as Grisi, Taglioni, Legnani, Pavlova, Karsavina. In Imperial Russia there was a definite hierarchy of dancers, at the top of which was the *prima ballerina assoluta*, a title occasionally granted half a century ago, and still used in the U.S.S.R. to designate the highest ranking of several ballerinas. The renaissance fostered by Diaghilev has underwritten the proper definition for our time, and possibly a long time ahead, as a professional female dancer of the highest quality, gifted with authority, superlative stage-presence and looks.

There are today two English ballerinas: Markova and Fonteyn, both of indisputable quality which has been revealed and developed through unremitting work, and tested in a thousand performances. The one is a product of Russian-style training and of dancing experience in a Russian company; the other (apart from some early Russian-style training) is entirely a product of the Sadler's Wells school, whose experience has been acquired in modern English works and classical revivals. Markova is English by birth but not, strictly speaking, a ballerina of English ballet; Fonteyn is the ballerina raised within an English system of ballet and has worked inside a very narrow range of choreographic influences.

The technical qualifications of ballerina—the absorption and absolute mastery of the traditional classical dance style and an imaginative grasp of mime—can be achieved by five out of ten students who will apply themselves wholeheartedly to the task. But the highest positions are filled only by those who can strain every nerve towards the ideal of perfectly expressive dancing—who can, in fact, give every part of the personality to the task. This process of personal dedication, of entire subservience to the art and craft of dancing, can be effected only by the dancer with singleness of vision and uncompromising integrity concerning her work. Outside interests of every kind, including friendships, must be subsidiary to her dancing; leisure pursuits, sleep, diet, dress, exercise and relaxations must be regulated in deference to the daily training routine, to rehearsals, and, in season, to performances.

A potential ballerina does not have to qualify as a beauty to win her top ranking. A study of theatrical and cinematic physiognomy shows us that a quite ordinary assemblage of features is transformable into a beautiful face by expressive use in performance, i.e. through controlled movement.

There is perhaps some consolation in the (possibly apocryphal) story of Diaghilev's advice to Markova: that she needed only sufficient make-up to define the facial detail to the first few rows of the stalls for beyond that distance the face was unimportant—what was being done with the body was what counted.

All dancers, being only human, have limitations of some sort in their range of movement or their expressive capabilities. The mark of great dancing (repeatedly grand performances, not just the odd occasion of brilliance) is that the limitation is accepted, then analysed, then worked upon until it becomes transmuted into an ingredient of the personal style— a mannerism but not an affectation. All dancers have mannerisms: the bad ones are those which are imitated from other dancers' styles too sedulously, or which are obviously used to cover up defects of technique.

ALICIA MARKOVA
From *The Spectator,* 7 June, 1956.

For a few weeks Markova is to be seen as a guest artist with the Royal Ballet at Covent Garden: she has already danced *Giselle* and *Les Sylphides* and will shortly add *The Sleeping Beauty* to her limited—but so revealing—repertoire. No comparisons, invidious or otherwise, should be drawn between her performances and those of other reigning ballerinas. She is one of that short list of top names in a profession whose higher echelons have always been (must always be) very sparsely populated. Like the other great ballerinas, she is unique, and therefore any performance in which she appears is a theatregoing experience of a high order.

Today, big-scale ballet has invented its own style of vulgarised publicity in all countries; its 'vital statistics' don't refer to that branch of numerology that so much preoccupies the world of lighter entertainment; they centre on the total of alleged ballerinas that any worthwhile company is able to muster. In fact, at even the lowest level of valuation of 'ballerina,' there are fewer than thirty to be found today topping the ranks of the twelve leading European and American ballet companies. A further handful, of which Markova is the *doyenne,* freelances around the globe, picking and choosing engagements in Melbourne, Rio, Chicago or London. Today, ballerinas are rarer than first-grade violin virtuosi, clear-thinking politicians and film actresses.

Markova herself probably cares less than anyone else that it is known she is within a few months in age of Ulanova: the history books are packed with details of her earliest seasons with Diaghilev, back in the days just after the First World War. All that matters is that, even in a list of ballets fewer than the symphonies of Beethoven, she dances to reveal a complete and totally individualised version of the character portrayed, and in a style for which the word is 'miraculous'. This is no place for analysis of how she acquired, and maintains, that style; it came to full realisation during her wartime years with Ballet Theatre in America. For the past twelve years she has been showing a kind of dancing more refined (in the cleanest sense of the word) than anything else now on view on any stage.

This refinement results in an effortlessness—an air of utterly spontaneous creation of the role—that provides a double visual pleasure: first, the artless smoothness, the melting of one phrase of movement into the next, and secondly, the sharpening of our awareness of the nuances of tempo, her use of *rubato*, the thistledown lightness which has so positive a quality. It looks so simple that one realises (possessing even the slenderest knowledge of any dance technique) its simplicity is compounded of layer upon layer of disciplines regarding weight, equilibrium, timing, extension, contraction, so that the dance utterance has the condensation, the supernormal stylisation and the impact of a great lyric poem.

## MARGOT FONTEYN
From *Ballet Today*, April, 1956.

The 10th anniversary of the postwar re-opening of the Royal Opera House was marked by a performance of *The Sleeping Beauty*—so far as possible, identical in cast with the initial performance of 20 February, 1946. In fact, there were three dancers appearing in the same rôles on these two dates ten years apart—Margot Fonteyn, Beryl Grey, Leslie Edwards; less than a dozen soloists still survive from that first performance and the main solid core of the Company now consists of dancers who were at that time either corps-de-ballet members or still in the student stage.

This is inevitable, and possibly this company has as high a reputation as any other top-rank company in the world today, as a place in which dancers stay, and continue to stay, through the changes and vicissitudes of the years. But one regrets the moving on of some notable dancers who were with the company in its early Covent Garden days; dancers who have not yet ceased activity and who now dance elsewhere or work as teachers, producers and *régisseurs*.

Miss Fonteyn provided a red-letter day for all of us who recalled both the 1946 occasion and the first performance of the first production of this ballet, at Sadler's Wells in 1939. She has, at some indefinable point within the past three years, attained that degree of harmonious balance of all the parts of the personality, all the possible nuances of interpretation of the character, all the finesse that the actual technique involved will permit; and this blend of qualities she now projects in each performance of those rôles which she feels are incontestably hers. (It is perhaps superfluous to point out that a dancer of her quality and status does not undertake rôles which do not fully involve her interest; indeed why should a talent of this size be wasted on characterisations thin enough to be adequately performed by junior ballerinas, even soloist dancers?)

What becomes more and more obvious with this repertoire is the fact that the 19th century full-length ballets are *not* merely ballerina-vehicles; although a good deal of their choreography suggests that the Old Masters who created them took their contemporary ballerinas very seriously (understandable when the records show that the said ballerinas would not hesitate to intrigue against any choreographer who failed to create big dance parts for them in his more important new works). In spite of the deficiencies—and they *are* deficiencies despite what the fashionable apologists for ballet pretend—of long, shapeless ensembles, of insipid solos, of mime-action of a staggering, moronic level, nevertheless these ballets, such as *Swan Lake, The Sleeping Beauty, Coppélia, Giselle,* contain enough lively dance moments, little passages of mime, phases of manoeuvring of varying sized choral groups, to be worth all our attention. The ballerina's own performance is heightened and intensified by the general high quality attained by the rest of the cast.

The paradox of ballet in performance is that second-rate work all round *does not* provide a flattering framework for the ballerina-rôle; in a lazy performance the ballerina's effort looks unduly strained, the technique shows through the "skin" of the part. Whereas if the whole cast works to create clean, strong dancing and miming, it develops an atmosphere of full commitment to the story which sustains and encourages the ballerina —even without her conscious awareness of what is happening—to give splendidly and completely everything she can live and feel and imagine into the central rôle.

The test, on both the company and the other top-rank dancers, of giving five further performances of this work in succession proved too much for everybody. Against all one's human (and critical) inclinations, one was compelled to judge the other exponents of the Aurora rôle by contrasting them against Fonteyn's performance. This is an inevitability with a company making a big policy point of keeping these ancient works in active repertoire, to this considerable extent. Violetta Elvin and Beryl Grey make highly individual, and legitimate, interpretations of Aurora, but with them there goes a stronger stress on different parts of each act, of each big scene, of each dance, and Fonteyn's superb ability is to extract the last milligramme of expressiveness out of both her acting and her dancing in *every second* of every phase of the ballet.

# IV

# *Foreign Ballet*

# Foreign Ballet

## THE BOLSHOI BALLET IN LONDON (1956)

Compiled from notices in *The Spectator*, *Ballet Today* and *The Daily Telegraph*, October and November, 1956.

The long-awaited, almost-abandoned, thunderously acclaimed, opening performance of the Bolshoi Theatre Ballet in London on 3 October provided ammunition for the arguers of every imaginable point of view about the excellence, oddity, dullness or strangeness of modern Soviet ballet—compared with modern Western ballet. No previous foreign dance company appearing in London has ever required that its work be judged by its own standards so clearly as is necessary on this occasion. All idealistic chatter about Art being international apart, there is not more than one square foot of common ground shared by Soviet and non-Soviet ballet companies today. They have a common parentage, an inherited tradition of a classical dance-mode (mainly formulated and taught world-wide by French and Italian masters for 200 years), and a shared heritage of a handful of romantic-style ballets dating from about a century ago. But the separation between Russia and the rest of the world which was effected when Diaghilev and Fokine made their reformation in 1909 in Paris became a complete severance by the time of the Revolution. Soviet ballet has become a different kind of art in the Russian theatre; every one of its components has been analysed, compared, and dialectically argued into (or out of) existence in exactly the same way that all the other arts have been overhauled, reshaped and given new ideological dress in recent years.

Diaghilev's reformation was based on the Fokine type one-act ballet—now the norm of Western balletmaking everywhere—which supposedly demands a fresh, clear-cut choreographic style for each fresh subject and requires that style to be illuminated and sustained by appropriate music, décor and staging; possibly as many as 2,000 one-act ballets have been made—outside Russia—since 1906. Soviet ballet is a repertoire of ancient and modern full-length ballets; a totally comprehensive training system involving general, artistic and dance education; a meticulously preserved attitude towards past Russian achievements (the great ballets of the

89

nineteenth century); and a cultural force, within Russia, probably as weighty as the nation's drama or literature.

The two first productions were *Romeo and Juliet* and *Swan Lake*, neither completely novel sensations. We in this country have had full-length versions of *Swan Lake* for some years and most ballet-addicts have seen the Soviet film version of *Romeo and Juliet*, with many of the same dancers.

But when the curtain rose on *Romeo and Juliet* on Wednesday, 3 October, all despair vanished, most doubts were killed. One might not like the new Soviet choreography, one could (perhaps) shudder at the realistic scenery—but there was no doubt that the Soviet system produces *dancers*. Later, as the performance developed and Ulanova's magic began to work (even upon those most disappointed with the décor and the choreographic structure) we were aware of watching the results of a completely new conception of ballet. At almost no point does it resemble the Western idea of what ballet is for: how it is best made: what kind of subjects are most suitable: what kind of personality the dancer should acquire in order to realise the character most completely.

*Romeo and Juliet* tells Shakespeare's story in terms of dramatic dance-and-mime with clarity and great emotional impact; it compresses those incidents of the play which do not dynamically advance the plot, though nothing of significance is omitted.

The choreography is the special development that has taken place in Russia since the 1920s, out of the common heritage that all European theatres shared during the 19th century. It has a smaller vocabulary than is in use here with mainly big, open steps and gestures; there are few of those subtle, refined head-hand-and-arm movements that make up most of the Western choreographer's apparatus. But the ballet, remarkable as a translation of a great poetic play into a wordless spectacular narrative, demands a lot of large-scale, heroic crowd scenes and ensembles. By contrast the solo or duet dances have to have a simplicity and brevity which make them most moving in effect.

The 19th century realistic style of the décor, with costumes owing nothing to this century's revolutions in either fashion or stagecraft, is exactly in keeping with the choreographic style; its designs are almost unaltered copies of costumes, architecture and furnishings from 16th century Italian painting. In these settings the crowd scenes have a powerful excitement, similar to the best parts of Russian and Italian films of silent days. This Verona is a plausible one, though its atmosphere carries a hint of Northern coolness and does not quite convince us of Southern sunshine.

The enormous cast appeared absolutely at ease, dancing and miming with effortless control and assurance. The orchestra did not seem perfectly happy with Prokofiev's score, which, however, in itself has a good deal of repetition and some dull passages.

The real impact of the occasion was the splendidly simple quality of Ulanova's dancing and personality. On her first appearance as Juliet she revealed that she is an absolute dancer; as the story unfolded in riot and rout, in gambol and duel, she showed herself incontestably one of the very great dancers of our day. Her lightness conceals disciplined strength, her movement is never forced, hard or obvious; she flows into and out of the dance phrases as artlessly and beautifully as a bird flies or a fish swims. Her Juliet *was* the child of a Renaissance house who met, adored, wedded and lost a noble and devoted youth; the Romeo of Yuri Zhdanov was on nearly the same level of acting ability and, as partner, in perfect unison with Ulanova at every moment. At an age when most ballerinas retire she commands the art that enables her to create the perfect theatrical illusion —she *is* Juliet, not the performer, and her dancing translates the simple choreography into a moving theatrical event.

*Swan Lake* is an entirely fresh re-arrangement of the old choreography of Gorsky (the Moscow régisseur who made a complete revision of the Petipa-Ivanov version in 1911), with additions by Messerer and Radunsky. The story is almost precisely the same as in our familiar versions but the dance incidents each vary either in duration or choreographic shape—or both. The big change is in the finale of the fourth act; instead of hero and heroine having to embrace death as the only solution of their plight, here they are happily united, the Magician's spell over Odette is broken and she and Siegfried become—as in many another good fairytale—a happy-ever-after couple.

Generally the dances are simpler in shape, using fewer of the traditional steps, gestures and poses. But these elements are here assembled in different rhythms and stage patterns with a notable difference of dramatic and lyric effect. This Moscow *Swan Lake* is, to non-Russian eyes, quite fairy-tale in quality by the *obvious* simplicity of its story-telling and of its characterisation. The décor of Virsaladze has affinities with our dramatic theatre of the 1900s—naturalistic in style and with a colour range appropriate to respectable Academy painting of that day.

One of the company's younger talents, Nina Timofeyeva, appeared as Odette-Odile. Her interpretation in Act 2 seemed cool and remote some of the time, this sensation being sweepingly overridden by the passionate feeling she conveyed at the high dramatic moments. Act 3, the ballroom scene, gave her occasion to scintillate in a choreography whose verve and brilliance are outstanding in comparison with any other production. She achieved this despite slight nervousness, doubtless due to the solemn occasion.

The *divertissement* dances here showed the Russians' unimpaired mastery of all kinds of dance styles of folk basis. In this act also Nikolai Fadeyechev as Siegfried showed his paces as a virtuoso in further novel and exciting choreography.

All through, the ballet seemed rather slower-paced than do other versions; the acting and miming were less obvious; more of the story's impact was carried through the actual dancing. Yet the total impact was an unhappy one. Possibly this modern version of a 19th century success is too different—not inferior or superior—in expressive power compared with Western versions.

With the addition of the two later ballets (*The Fountain of Bakhchisarai* and *Giselle*) to its London repertoire, the Bolshoi Ballet presented further opportunities for measuring the details which constitute the unique quality of contemporary Russian achievement. Two 'classics' and two modern works, each distinct from its partner in the same category, show a wide range of choreographic, dancing and production modes—sufficient to permit one to dare assess the creative and the possibly retardative factors in present-day ballet-making in Moscow.

The standard of actual dance performance—precisely what flows out of each performer's heart, mind and body into the shape and style and rhythm of the movements—is on the same high level, and of the same intensity of projection, as was revealed in the first few performances of the opening week. The appurtenances of dancing (the décor, music, staging, choreography) in *The Fountain of Bakhchisarai* were of varying quality, and only the miraculous level of interpretation could save the ensemble of parts from degenerating into fourth-rate ballet of a kind not often found among European companies.

The Pushkin theme is excellent dance-drama material; a Tartar savage leads his horde against a Polish outpost, which is obliterated, and only a captive maid survives to be enrolled in the Khan's harem. But her beauty and her indifference to him rouse the not-unnoble savage to wonder at, then to fall in love with, her. His cast-off wife in a jealous fit kills the maid; the Khan sinks into even profounder gloom; his ever-conquering warriors returning from more raids cannot enliven him. The ex-wife is unceremoniously tossed over the battlements and the Khan retires to mourn over the fountain he has erected in honour of the noble maiden.

This bare outline of the story can only slightly indicate the range and intensity of the dance and mime incidents forming the ballet.

The story runs in four acts, two of exact dramatic duration and persuasive power, two of them padded with overmuch waiting and watching for incidents which, when developed, are too brief to win all our sympathy.

Maria, the captive maid, was played with a warmly lyric sensibility by Raissa Struchkova. Zarem was a role danced and acted with nicely controlled bravura by Velta Viltsin. The Khan, an unbelievably difficult rôle to fulfil, acted throughout almost entirely on one note of noble frustrated passion, was carried off triumphantly by Alexander Lapauri. He made a most noble savage, convincing in stature of both heart and mind.

The ceremonial and martial incidents of Act 1 are based on military and pastoral dances of Polish origin. These and the splendidly naturalistic fights around the burning manor house made a theatricality of high order, a compelling realism of effect of a kind long lost to our theatre. The court scene had some lovely moments but its general effect was of a choreography of limited power. This drama is an unbalanced one, too much of minor interest occurring between the fine climactic moments. The ballet suffers from an excess of that naturalism which is such a virtue in *Romeo and Juliet*. Had its choreography been as precise as were the Pushkin verses on which it is based, *The Fountain of Bakhchisarai* could be reckoned a balletic masterpiece. Its diffuseness and the mediocrity of its score by Asafiev are only partly compensated for by the best of the choreography—even the truly magnificent Tartar war dance of the finale.

*Giselle,* however, is, for the present season, the triumph of the Company. This old romantic tragedy came theatrically alive as though it were being performed for the first time ever—a tribute to Lavrovsky's subtle and splendidly imagined reconstruction of both story and choreography, and also to the unbelievable transformation of Ulanova's personality *into* the heroine. No such dancing by anyone of any nationality, status or length of experience has happened before in my thirty years of London balletgoing.

The story of the oldest surviving ballet is, with a few variations of detail, told exactly as in non-Russian versions. There are small neat stresses on characterisation here and there, and a few points of the action which must be made unequivocally clear are accented afresh. The choreography is a noble tribute not only to the 19th century masters who made and remade it (Coralli, Perrot and Petipa), but also to Lavrovsky, who has meticulously worked upon it to give it the maximum intensity of expressiveness.

The perfection of Ulanova's dance-acting is in every sense incomparable —that is, not to be measured by any standard applying to other dancers. She is the standard, the absolute, emotion-crammed essence of the tragic character. In one sense we were seeing the ballet *Giselle* for the first time; previously we have seen productions of it. It was the creation of the whole work, even though the calendar says that it is 115 years since Grisi first danced it.

How much the occasion gained its intensity from the choreography and how much from Ulanova's ability to create, and retain unshakeably, the character, is debatable and not of the least importance. These two constituents work together; a great artist is presented within a faultless framework and the result is "theatre" of the highest intensity.

It is, perhaps, a test of one's artistic feeling or else an exercise in self-discipline, to have to look at these ballets (and these dancers) without in any way comparing them with the works and personalities already known to us. This is difficult and, for some people, impossible; yet only by looking with fresh, clear eyes can we see the significance of contemporary Soviet ballet, as revealed here.

There is no such thing as "The Greatest Ballerina In The World"; there are a number of great dancers of ballerina rank in several countries, and the acknowledged leading one of each race or nation is she who most comprehensively and most continuously *creates* the characters she dances, probably in a wide variety of ballets. Differences of physique and nervous sensibility create vast differences between their performing styles: different methods of schooling and the occurrence or absence of opportunity to dance often enough to satisfy the performer's creative power and appetite will make significant contributions to her prowess as a ballerina. Of course, the spectator who confines his interest to one ballerina will never be able to measure her gifts accurately—however splendid she may be for him, he can never fairly calculate whether she is a greater dancer than any other of the same rank.

Then again, there is only a small repertory of ballets known to and danced regularly by different ballerinas; and this is another factor working against the honest assessment of the talents of several ballerinas. An interest in the art of ballet, an interest in the craft and mystique of dancing, encourage the spectator to watch different performers giving clearly differing interpretations, allowing him to taste several kinds of aesthetic and emotional effect—provided the performances are danced and acted with complete sincerity and commitment.

All the ballerinas I can number at this moment vary in age (and therefore in experience) and in the quality and depth of their emotional projection on stage; some no longer dance certain roles they once performed, and many of them have not danced—and possibly never will dance—roles which others can create into splendid characterisations. All this is to suggest that comparisons between Ulanova, Struchkova and other Russian ballerinas, and their Western counterparts, are more or less meaningless. These Russians can produce a kind of effect we have rarely, if at all, met before: but then their attitude towards ballet is completely different from that of Western dancers.

If this vast difference can be assessed and stated in a few words, it seems to be: in Russia, ballet has been manipulated so that it is, within their culture, a major art, not a minor one as it has always been in Europe. Part of this process of re-thinking ballet into a new shape has been the development of a style of dance-acting based on the discipline, close study of the role, and finely balanced team-work, that emanate from the Stanislavsky method of actor-training. In addition, their choreographers have analysed every second of the action (whether planned, as for a new ballet, or existing, as in an old ballet—*Swan Lake,* for instance). They have then ruthlessly trimmed, clarified, adjusted, or simplified it so that the continuous action of any phase of any ballet—whether five seconds or five minutes in length—never fails to open out the plot, reveal significant aspects of the characters, or in some way keep the spectators' attention riveted on the continuous unfolding of the story. Without making any unjust comparisons with Western ballets, it is obvious that this concentration on keeping the ballet going as the unfolding of a meaningful story is something that the Russians can do consummately well.

Again, our development of ballet for forty-odd years has been along the lines of Fokine's principles and we have been ensnared by, as well as legitimately fascinated by, the formula of the one-act, short ballet. We have made a kind of ballet which must necessarily have scenery, costumes, music, staging, and dance-style in key with the theme or idea or plot— which accounts for all the cleverness, the touches of genius, and the banality, repetitiveness and vulgarity that one sees in so many works by Western choreographers today.

This only partly touches upon the big, basic differences between Soviet and non-Soviet ballet-making today; each side can find things to inspire, amaze or horrify it in the other's ballet system; and each has quite a lot to teach the other if only the right bridges between the two systems can be found and used. Neither can expect to be wholly successful with the spectators of the other system, because the systems themselves differ in being artistic expressions of two wholly different social structures . . .

Given an understanding that these differences do exist, we can accept and at the same time reject many things in these Bolshoi ballets.

The intense manner of dance-acting plus the fruits of that academic method they have been perfecting for over two hundred years imbue the dancers with a sense of devotion to the act of performance that produces effortless, unstrained, fully extrovert dancing. The men mostly appear more muscular, more masculine than ours but lack their grace, delicacy and courtliness; they dance effortlessly with a greater range of movements which they execute with more fire, athleticism and passion than do Western dancers.

The naturalistic sets and costumes, which upset so many people, logically fit the Russian conception of décor as, literally, merely a background for the dancing—not a contributory factor to the atmosphere of the story.

No dancer appearing in any role, however small, failed to dance and act all-out—that is, sincerely but without obvious "showmanship". After the ballerinas Ulanova, Struchkova, Karelskaya and Timofeyeva, one can only record the faultless characterisations and dance performances of the leading males in leading roles—Fadayechev as Albrecht and Siegfried; Kondratov as Waclaw in *The Fountain of Bakhchisarai,* Zhdanov, Koren and Rikhter in *Romeo and Juliet,* and Lapauri in *Romeo* and *Bakhchisarai.* Yuri Faier, chief conductor, gets more out of the scores than one had thought possible . . . and these notes are no more than a brief summary of the unusual, disquieting, satisfying, thrilling and always highly memorable sensations induced by the opening performances of each of these four Soviet ballets.


## RUSSIAN BALLET IN THE MAKING (1960)

From *The Daily Telegraph,* 15 June, 1960.

Outside the Bolshoi Theatre a ticketless mob waves handfuls of grubby paper roubles. Another black market, you imagine, for have you not just been asked whether you have any foreign currency to sell?

But the ticket-sellers are not all sharks; some are secretaries of clubs, unions or school groups whose allocation has not been taken up. They come to sell tickets at marked prices so that they will not be wasted.

This seems to me less a comment on Russian morality than evidence of regard for "our Bolshoi". The same thing happens at the other Moscow ballet theatre, the Stanislavsky, and at the two Leningrad theatres.

These ballet-and-opera theatres are unique, though not quite in the way the Russians have been taught. The special quality of Russian ballet grows out of a thoroughness of training, a high level of theatre craft, ingenuity of production and staging, all of which are stimulated by a public appetite for good theatre.

When Russian ballet came to the European capitals early in this century it showed that the Russians were, in this field, world-beaters. The Diaghilev Ballet, with its novel productions and fresh notions of music, theme and designing, and with such stars as Karsavina, Pavlova and Nijinsky, offered ballet as a serious theatre art just when Europeans generally were beginning to take the theatre seriously again. It was the main inspiration of the ballet revival that has swept round the world in the past forty years.

Under the Soviet régime ballet has followed a different path. What can be seen in Russia now shows far less experiment than elsewhere.

Sixteen days spent in watching performances, classes and rehearsals, and in discussions with teachers, directors and choreographers of ballet companies in Moscow and Leningrad have provided answers, even though incomplete ones, to many questions about the Russian ballet of today. How does it differ from ours, and why? Have the Russians lessons for us, and we for them?

The main difference is that ballet, like all theatre arts in Russia, is amply subsidised. The quality of the training, the splendour of production and the complete professionalism demanded of the dancers are achieved in conditions where there are no worries about money or security, and no need for artists to over-work.

Another difference is that most of the repertoire consists of full-length works, and this has encouraged choreographic and performing conditions putting great emphasis on dance-acting rather than on dancing pure and simple. At their best, the Russians can give truly great interpretations of such 19th century works as *Giselle, Swan Lake* and *The Sleeping Beauty*. On another level, they present ballets which no amount of fine acting, dancing and stagecraft can bring to artistic life, for their themes are too crudely propagandist. Yet I felt that the audiences swallowed the themes without noticing much, and concentrated on the virtuosity of their favourites.

The scale is vast compared with all other places; stages, companies, orchestras are bigger, and ballets employ all the devices of lighting, décor and production to make every sort of stage illusion. Scenery almost invariably is closely naturalistic, with every leaf on a tree, every brick in a wall, looking utterly lifelike.

If much of this strikes the Western spectator as naïve, any feeling of superiority is soon dispersed by the quality of performance. You feel that these real leaves and feathers and jewels and furniture are the proper trimmings for the style of dancing and acting, which, nearly always, has that magical quality of seeming quite spontaneous.

The composer is the idol of the Soviet ballet world—not, as with us, the choreographer—and conductors really study ballets and a dancer's needs, and have very big orchestras to command. The two big theatres, the Moscow Bolshoi and the Leningrad Kirov, have ninety men in the pit.

But all this great apparatus is firmly based on the dancers' craft. The Soviet régime scarcely touched the ballet training system of Czarist days; only the scale is altered. Between 1738 and 1918 the numbers of students in Moscow and St Petersburg did not exceed one hundred, but by now students and staff have trebled in each school. Training is free, and lasts nine years; there is a six-year course for dancers who specialise in folk-dance, revues and drama productions.

Picked by a large panel of teachers and dancers, the young pupil enters into a life almost monastic in its simplicity and severity. He receives a general education, studies music and theatre history as well as dancing, and learns to be one of a community devoted to the idea of serving the theatre for a lifetime. He acquires self-discipline and has to follow the rules. I was impressed by the firm but not harsh discipline in both Moscow and Leningrad.

The training is tough, with a timetable running from 8.30 a.m. to late afternoon six days a week. Quite early, children are gradually introduced to the stage by walking on, or simply being part of a background crowd. Pupils come from all parts of the Soviet Union, and in both schools there are more children looking like Asians than like Russians. You could easily cast all of *Flower Drum Song* or a revival of *Chu Chin Chow* out of a Russian dance school.

With a wastage rate of fifteen per cent., there are about thirty-five graduates each summer in each city, and this year there are nearly a hundred jobs to fill, For the ballet-and-opera theatres in Tashkent, Baku, Kazan, Tiflis, Alma-Ata and a dozen other cities want recruits from Moscow and Leningrad to stiffen the local talent.

Pay rates cannot easily be compared with those outside, but a *corps-de-ballet* beginner with 1,000 roubles monthly is not worse off than his or her London counterpart. Soloists earn about 2,500 roubles, and a top-rating ballerina will have 6,000 roubles plus many amenities. (Much unskilled labour has a basic rate of 450 roubles.)

So the dancer in Russia has a secure job and has been finely trained for it. But from our viewpoint is all this care and sound organisation justified by the end-product? Sixty years after Fokine and Gorsky Russian ballet remains remarkably as it was in 1900. Choreography—the actual pattern of steps and gestures—has a much smaller vocabulary than here. The great 19th-century ballets have been pulled to pieces and reproduced over and over, to achieve a greater degree of "naturalness" in the character-isation—a style of creative performance such as these dancers, and only these, can show.

Ballet in Russia has, I believe reached its limit of expressiveness in its present form; and not much freshness can be induced until a lot of Western achievement has been shown there. With the regular introduction of theatre works from abroad Russian choreographers, critics and dancers will see that our use of ballet as, primarily, an entertainment with lyrical, dramatic or comic undertones is a splendid form of theatre.

In all my discussions I felt more and more sure that the directors and choreographers and artists know that we in the West have achieved much by our endless experiments with the short form of ballet. They are interested in what they call "pure dance" (ballets which do *not* have to tell a story) and, now and then, some one makes a programme of such *miniatures*, as they are termed, in a mode that, outside Russia, has produced something like 1,000 worthwhile short ballets since 1910.

Perhaps the best means of broadening their view would be visits by the best Danish, English and American ballet companies, in that order, showing ballets closest to and farthest away from the formulas now in use in Russia. These companies' vast range of styles in dancing, use of music and design could provide a textbook of what non-Russian ballet has been doing for over a century.

If the Russians are interested in learning from us, this is the finest lesson we could offer. We also could learn much from their training system by introducing some of their meticulously detailed dance instruction.

Some Russians, at any rate, are looking for new ways in the arts. At the British painting exhibition in Moscow a young Leningrad poet, defending the modernist works, said to me: "There must not always be 'literature' (he meant social messages) on top of painting and music and ballet. Do you understand me?" I understood perfectly.

## DANCERS ACROSS THE CURTAIN (1961)

From *The Daily Telegraph*, 15 July, 1961.

If cultural exchanges are to result in their maximum usefulness, both Russians and English must be willing to admit that their systems of ballet have important lessons for each other. While the Kirov Ballet from Leningrad has been dancing here at Covent Garden, the Royal Ballet has visited Leningrad and Moscow.

Little hard news has yet reached here about Russian reactions to our style of dancing and our kinds of ballets; certainly the opening performances in both cities were a triumph, as they are bound to be when a famous foreign company packed with novelty appears anywhere for the first time.

Even if a majority of Russians—particularly the professionals of ballet —found our varieties of choreography novel and even startling, it is not very likely that they will emulate the styles of Ashton, de Valois, MacMillan or Cranko in a hurry. Cautiousness, expressed in a thorough dialectical analysis of Western ballet's ways-and-means, will permit choreographic experiment at only a minimal rate.

The impact of the Kirov Ballet here has been a curious one. The casual public has frequently found itself surprised and thrilled by the company's best dancing, though it has not escaped notice that the dramatic element (mainly expressed in full-toned, extrovert acting) is less obvious than in our own types of ballet.

Indeed, for the English ballet-conscious public, the season has been a glorious revelation—of a quality of interpretation of characters and of dance-style quite unlike anything shown here by Russian dancers since, one imagines, the first visit of Diaghilev's company in 1911.

Not that there is much common ground for comparisons; the ballets are different and so are the qualities of décor and stagecraft. But certainly what we have been seeing this past month suggests that there has continued, throughout these fifty years, that same kind of sensuous elegance, of pure simplicity of movements, that record says was one of the strongest sensations felt half a century ago. The St Petersburg style has simply changed title to the Kirov style.

It is worth noting the impact nearly five years ago of the Bolshoi Ballet from Moscow, when it appeared here. Its visit bore the cachet of two splendid "firsts"—the company's first full-scale appearance in any

Western capital and the West's first view of the talent of Ulanova. No dancer since Pavlova was preceded by such fame, and Ulanova fully justified all that had been said.

But if one quality more than any other in the Bolshoi company's interpretations, in ballets both old and new, surprised us with its difference, it was the dynamic projection of their style of dance-acting. The biggest surprise (and one of pleasure) from the Kirov company, on the other hand, has been a lack of this forceful quality: instead they have invested everything they perform with a refined lyricism, an effortless simplicity, such as we have seen from no other dance group in the world.

Probably it is this illusion of simplicity which has made such an appeal to us, for the best of our dramatic acting (particularly in the great interpretations of classical plays, like Gielgud or Olivier in *Hamlet*) has carried this signature: our kind of ballet has a long way yet to go to acquire this apparent inevitability.

Of course the ballets given by the Kirov company have not been altogether faultless. *The Stone Flower* wears a propagandist message a little too obviously on its sleeve; their *Giselle* seems to many English observers to lack the vigorous dramatic passages necessary to justify its lurid plot. Many items in the mixed bill, *Gala Programme,* were trivial—even when impeccably danced.

By Western standards, ballet in Soviet Russia simply has not yet begun to exploit all those tricks, refinements, experiments in stagecraft, in lighting, in scenery and costume that our theatre has used as common currency for forty years past.

One splendid exception here: Virsaladze's designs for the Kirov *Sleeping Beauty* were a masterpiece of cunning simplicity. He had planned every piece of scenery, every costume, to achieve its desired effect in the simplest fashion, so that no extraneous, noticeable detail even momentarily detracted from the ease and clarity of the dancing. Never have I seen dancers' bodies so ideally clad to reveal and illuminate every posture, gesture, step or transitional movement.

Perfectly in key with the company's status relative to the Bolshoi company, it did not come packed with "star names" we have been hearing of for years. But then, Moscow has been the magnet for all visitors to Russia for 40 years past: Leningrad is thought of as a backwater.

So the most promising Kirov school talents were sooner or later taken to Moscow, as guests, many of them later to be persuaded that Moscow was the more important centre for making a career. Ulanova was a Leningrad graduate and started her career there.

During their two months here and in Paris, the Kirov Company's leading dancers have made for themselves considerable Western reputations. We must hope that this will not go unnoticed in Moscow when the company returns home. Six dancers of "ballerina size"—Osipenko, Moiseyeva, Kolpakova, Gensler, Sizova, and Kekisheva—have given us dancing, suave, delicate and precise, that has almost invariably justified that surprising adjective "aristocratic", while Soloviev proves to be a male dancer worth calling phenomenal.

While London has been showing an absolutely spontaneous gratitude for these dancers, Russia has reacted to the Royal Ballet in warm—if seemingly, cautious—terms.

Both *Ondine* and *La Fille mal gardée* had ecstatic receptions in Leningrad. Margot Fonteyn was judged "very elegant", "amazing because of her exceptional charm and purity of line", and she "impressed by her feeling, high skill and sincerity". A veteran Moscow critic in a recent letter says: "Her dancing sings, her body is exceptionally expressive and she is a marvellous actress".

Yet anyone acquainted with our Royal Ballet and the two top Russian companies can see worlds of difference in their work. Each set of dancers fits (or is fitted to) its kind of ballets, but also we know that Russians could expand the appeal of their ballet by using our sorts of choreographic experiment. Conversely, we have room to develop our dancers' basic movement styles tenfold if we could absorb some of the Russian methods of teaching technique, of training for stage work, and of inducing in dancers some of the passionate commitment that the Russians have for their careers.

Exchange visits of companies open eyes on both sides of the Curtain, but real interchange of artistic know-how can come only by parties from both sides working in the other's system. We might achieve things if Russia would send a dozen top teachers for a minimum of five years.

The same length of time would be about enough to enable four or five of our best choreographers to introduce into the Russian system a new view of what ballet is for. They could show the effects to be got by using dancing to comment on, illustrate and even beautify all those absurd and wonderful activities in which human beings can indulge.

There is more to dancing than merely preaching the Heroism of Labour, or narrating the Unimportance of Being Earnest.

## THE KIROV BALLET IN LONDON (1961 and 1966)

These notices on the Kirov Ballet in London are edited from
those in *The Daily Telegraph* in June and July, 1961 and
September and October, 1966.

## 1961

The Kirov Ballet Company from Leningrad, once the Maryinsky, artistically the equal and historically the senior to the Bolshoi Company in
Moscow, opened its Covent Garden season last night* with *The Stone
Flower*, to Prokofiev's last score. Of all post-war ballets of Russian origin
seen here it most perfectly stresses the difference between audience-needs
in Russia and in the West. The story is based on a fable about a noble-
hearted pair of young lovers, a scheming villain and a supernatural visitant
who is, alternately, a benefactress, a seductress and also the *dea ex machina*
who sets all things right and brings everything to a happy ending. This
fable has been turned into a complex and highly professionally organised
ballet mainly to tell a story, with an obvious double meaning, to its native
public. Here we would be content to make a straight entertainment of it
and any philosophic afterthoughts could be concocted by the audience
for themselves.

Undoubtedly on its home ground this tale of a young artisan seeking to
become an artistic creator, sustained through calamity and trial by the pure
love of his village sweetheart, tempted by and resisting supernatural powers,
is laden with meanings which smoothly translate into terms of Socialist
Realism. This heavy load of symbolism, while not actually impeding the
choreographic flow, does permeate the action—to an extent that one sees
the ballet in, as it were, stereoscopic vision.

The dance and action of a scene quite often impress with their beauty
and dynamism but, most of the time, they have to be simultaneously
interpreted as phases in the hero's struggle for enlightenment, as aspects of
the villain's evil character, or as a comment on the idyllic simplicity and
innocence of the young heroine.

The exceptions to this are, firstly, the Fairground Scene, which is a
brilliantly conceived suite of dance incidents with an almost symphonic
subtlety of structure and style. And most of the real-life crowd scenes,
pictures of village activity, have a similar choreographic excitement.

The "unreal" scenes—those inside the Copper Mountain where the
enchantress dwells—are frequently repetitive and use a limited vocabulary
of dance and mime.

*19 June, 1961

The visual contrast between the real world and the underworld is not sufficiently pictorially inventive: ideas of lighting and décor are almost primitive by our standards. The costumes and the movements for the spirit creatures, subjects of the Queen of the Copper Mountain, too much resemble some incidents in our own more pompous ballets of the 1930s.

The virtues of the production are the intense vitality of the dancing, the complete professionalism of the interpretations of the four principals and the aforesaid vividness and rousing theatricality of the big group numbers for the villagers. But they do not quite outweigh the long passages of repetitive dancing and the underlining.

These Leningrad dancers, in general, deploy a lighter and more suave style of classical dancing than their Moscow counterparts. On a first viewing they move lyrically rather than dramatically; sweetness and light are their characteristic dance overtones. Moscow has mainly shown us the heroic, the intense manner.

The solo dancing was unfailingly brilliant—often exciting. Yuri Soloviev as Danila, the hero, and Anatoli Gridin as the villainous Severian were superbly masculine and Russian—theatrical and professional to the tips of their finger nails.

In a difficult dance and acting idiom, Alla Osipenko as the underworld Queen gave a full realisation of the role. And Alla Sizova made an adorably sweet and wholly charming heroine.

The Kirov's *The Sleeping Beauty,* though not wholly perfect, was in many ways a revelation. The principal and most pleasurable surprise was for a non-Russian audience to be clearly shown what 19th century classical ballet really is and what it can be made to do.

Another helpful lesson—helpful because we have judged too much Soviet ballet décor by some fairly dreadful examples—was the setting and costumes here of Simon Virsaladze. He sets the work approximately at the close of the 17th century. The modest, pastel-dominated sets at first seem just so-so, suitable but unexciting. Only when the performance begins to unfold this fairy-tale saturated with a thousand years of European folklore do we realise that every brush-stroke in the scenery, every stitch of the costumes, is made to reveal, display and indirectly illuminate the movement quality of every dancer throughout.

The story is closer than Western versions to the original scenario and to Tchaikovsky's score. This allows the dramatic pace of the original legend to unfold steadily. It is this smooth telling of the story (where Western productions have built in too much fussy detail and empty choreography) which allows the interpreters of Aurora and the Prince to give us whole and highly effective characterisations.

The two final scenes have less impact, largely because by then choreographic inventiveness (by both Petipa, the ballet's creator, and Sergeyev, author of this revival) has thinned out, except for the betrothal *pas-de-deux* for Aurora and her Prince.

If any more exquisite interpretation of the role of Princess Aurora than that of Irina Kolpakova has occurred during my lifetime—well, I have missed it: and after seeing her I am content that this should be so.

This Aurora was such a complete and delicious interpretation throughout most of the action that we can forgive while regretting the few slight flaws that occurred in the final scene; and possibly less-than-perfect partnering was the cause of these. Miss Kolpakova looked and moved, from her first entrance and for two whole acts, like some exquisite gold-and-pink bird; and her dancing is of the phenomenal category.

Give or take a few hours and it is now just 120 years since *Giselle* was first performed in Paris*. Since then its position as the archetype of the supernatural, lyrical ballet of the great Romantic Age has never really been challenged. The production at Covent Garden last night by the Kirov Ballet suggested many reasons for its long survival, the most obvious being its completely theatrical exposition of plot and character. The Giselle was Irina Kolpakova, with Vladilen Semenov as Count Albrecht and Inna Korneyeva as the Queen of the Wilis.

The production plainly bears the stamp of the whole present Leningrad trend of both production and dance-and-acting method; a sense of cool effortlessness, smoothly elegiac acting and the extraction of every last milligramme of stylishness from the purely technical dancing.

This version is full of differences from Western productions. The Act I ensembles have less dancing; the business of establishing and confirming Count Albrecht's double life is more thoroughly detailed here and the larger patterns of group dances in both acts differ from ours.

All this adds up to a conclusion that this was no overwhelmingly dramatic occasion; there were some disappointments, and the final impact was of the telling of a gentle, melancholy fable, rather than of a thrillingly emotional drama.

Miss Kolpakova, who so exquisitely showed her highly personal ballerina-style in last week's production of *The Sleeping Beauty,* was a

*28 June, 1841

Giselle perfectly fitted to this production. Restraint, finesse and tenderness marked her interpretation and she makes fullest use of that kind of dance-acting at which Russian dancers are so adept. The line separating pure acting from pure dancing is almost impossible to see—which means that we strongly feel the impact of the marvellous mechanics of her movement and, as a secondary reaction, become aware of all those, as it were, minute brush-strokes with which she paints in the character's personality.

When she jumps, the take-off is utterly unstrained, and she returns to earth like a falling leaf or a November snowflake. Her sensitive touches of characterisation for this naïve young peasant are just as effortless and as astonishing.

Mr Semenov, not, on a second viewing, the most ideal partner for this Giselle, was an unlucky foil for her, his gesture and expression throughout being in a key different from hers.

Miss Korneyeva has, like Kolpakova, full control, especially in slow motion, of a formidable technique of jumps, extensions, and arabesques; the corps de ballet in Act II moved like thistledown. In sum, a performance delicately satisfying for those with a taste for the subtle, suave and serene.

If there is one classical ballet which the Kirov Company should perform surpassingly well it is the full-length *Swan Lake*. Their production inevitably evoked comparisons with others, for few companies in the world have the resources to stage this ballet comprehensively.

The original production in Moscow (1877) was a sad failure and it was the Kirov Company's predecessor—the Maryinsky Ballet, on which the first successful *Swan Lake* was created some years later. The present staging was almost totally lacking in dramatic force. None of the elements could create a focal point from which the rest of the action should radiate. Everything was interesting—but very little was exciting.

This production is a striking novelty for Western audiences, because of its "happy ending" twist to the story, its use of characters discarded in our versions and the considerable differences in the choreography.

Together with other Russian versions, this one fully uses the character of the Jester, Siegfried's personal attendant, here a brilliant performer (Alexandre Livshitz), but an irritating intruder into far too much of the action.

This character, together with the rather unconvincing presentation of Siegfried (by Vladilen Semenov) threw the production out of gear as much as anything else.

The famous and unusual lyric quality with which these Leningrad dancers invest their work was present in most of the ensembles and in all the secondary dancing roles. But it was allowed to melt away too often into imprecise figurings and too many soft accents.

Inna Zubkovskaya, the Odette-Odile character, is a formidable technician for the role and, given sharper production than here and a much more sympathetic partner for her Prince Siegfried, she could give an elegiac accenting to every phase. She has an obvious dramatic forcefulness but it was being kept on too tight a rein.

The brightest pleasure of the evening was, consistently, the dancing of the Swan groups in their many rich diversities of action and motion.

1966

The Kirov Ballet's second Covent Garden season has shown ballets varying from the sublime to the startlingly inept; happily, the marvels have outweighed the miseries.

One simple explanation exists for this variability; the administration of Soviet ballet pays more attention to the supposed needs of the home audience than it does to any aesthetic or philosophical concept of ballet. What started as an entertainment for aristocrats is nowadays carefully geared to make the maximum appeal to a public which is, artistically, the world's least sophisticated. Regretfully perhaps, we may say that an art for princes has been carefully scaled down into an art for peasants.

Nothing else explains Soviet tolerance for the poverty of such choreography as was seen in the Dwarfs episode and the unimaginative Prince's Journey scenes in *Cinderella*; and also in the divertissements *Walpurgisnacht*, *Prelude* and *The Blind Girl*, together with most of the excerpted *pas-de-deux* from full-scale ballets.

Yet when choreography of real quality was present the dancing has never been less than totally effortless, ecstatic in range and wonderful in its complete manipulation of the dancers. No other company can offer so much of the basic fascination of all stage dancing—the human form in patternings which create unique loveliness and therefore satisfy vicariously a universal need.

Deep down in the murk of each one's subconscious is an urge, hardly ever realised, to let ourselves run, jump, soar, float and spin; watching these dancers has given all of us, whether aware or not, that marvellous sense of release. But too many of the works are conceived as concentrated essays in circus effect. Circus effect is fine . . . inside circuses.

The makers of the dozen divertissements showed clearly their talent and its motivations; few of them missed a chance at the obvious, and only one, Vassily Vainonen, indicated that imaginative choreography is still possible under Soviet conditions.

The "problem" choreographer represented was Igor Belsky, whose *Leningrad Symphony* was a brave but not very successful attempt to create a ballet outside the traditional pattern. This work, inspired by the Siege of Leningrad (900 days of unrelieved hell), put the issue in black-and-white terms. Teutonic types invade and overwhelm the Soviet people, represented by young, resilient youths and maidens. Despite the numerical dominance of the invader the Russians resist and endure.

Political emotion dominates the ballet. (The fact that *Leningrad Symphony* is being performed in 1966 while a more potent political symbol is displayed in the Berlin Wall is due to no accident.) Its choreography is moulded (hand-sculptured, almost) out of Soviet glimpses of Western free-form dancing plus the ecstatic and distraught symbols found in traditional ballet movement.

Apart from the grandeur of an exquisite version of *The Sleeping Beauty* and the inevitable Soviet-style *Swan Lake* with a happy ending, the most complete revelation of all that this company has achieved (since ballet first entered Russia) was *Chopiniana*. More familiar to us as *Les Sylphides,* this was Fokine's earliest and most complete success and this production is the triumphal demonstration of the total refinement of classical dancing. Not only are form and content inextricably blended, but each illuminates and amplifies the other.

Every step, pose and position has been created so that the dancing speaks of purity and the god-aspiring nature of man. This was possible only because these dancers performed it with the blend of commitment and discipline that has grown out of a training still richly experimental even after 230 years' continuity.

To reduce this short season to its absolutely valuable elements; Fokine's masterpiece outweighed every folly in the rest of the repertoire; the dancing of the topmost echelon revealed, in every performance, discipline, simplicity and effortlessness. Their dancing had an inevitability of style that makes most non-Soviet dancing look too purposeful and strenuous.

While the Kirov Ballet continues to exist, no matter what our feelings about all other aspects of Soviet life, it can display a transcendental quality of ballet such as no other company in the world has yet even approximated.

As a postscript to the Kirov articles, this notice from
*The Daily Telegraph* is of Makarova's historic debut in *Giselle*, on
16 September, 1966.

The Kirov Ballet performance last night emphasised that success with a production of *Giselle* is not achieved simply through a sensitive interpretation of the title role.

The most bewitching of Giselles must be supported by fellow-artists of great talent, by wholly sympathetic dancing and by masterly production.

In this first performance this season at Covent Garden, Natalia Makarova displayed every qualification required for the leading role. As the peasant girl of Act I, she was tenderly charming and innocent, and ravishingly sweet in manner.

To the ghostly role of Act II, she brought a delicacy of movement that really seemed, as it should, unearthly. Her dancing had power without effort, sustained line and subtle accent without obviousness.

This sublime performer was matched with a fine dancing partner, Yuri Soloviev, whose acting only occasionally met the needs of the situation. As an adventuring, arrogant young prince he was convincing enough; but as a man discovering too late the ruin he had caused by his philandering, Mr Soloviev was insufficient.

In the Forest scene (Act II) he danced splendidly in support of and in contrast with Giselle, but the portrayal of a distracted youth paying retribution for his evil deeds lacked bigness of gesture and conviction of expression.

The corps de ballet, dynamic and unified yet nobly individual, brought telling emphasis to their ensembles in the choreography, here credited to Petipa, a reviser following the original creators.

Their beautiful execution of very simple steps and manoeuvres cunningly emphasised the choreographic symbolism of dark magic as expressed in complexities of mathematical patterning.

These episodes apart, much of the production lacked dramatic light and shade and had too many false pauses between plot-sequences.

Perfectly danced and acted interpretations by Anatoli Gridin as Hilarion (here titled "Hans") and Gabriella Komleva as Myrtha, together with the clean technical brilliance of Vadim Budarin in the Peasant *pas-de-deux,* were partial compensations for the missing balance in the leading roles.

## THE TWELFTH COPENHAGEN FESTIVAL (1961)

This article is compiled from *The Daily Telegraph* notices in
May and June, 1961.

3 June, 1961.

The permanently good things about the Royal Danish Ballet are such as to
justify—almost—the less-than-good-enough aspects of the 12th Copenhagen Festival just ended. Started in 1950 the festival is entirely national,
a series of special programmes drawn from the regular repertory of the
State theatres and national orchestras.

Next to the Russian, this is the world's most minutely-organised system
of dance training; it produces not simply good dancers but highly expressive dance-actors.

Ten ballets survive from the works of Auguste Bournonville (1805-
1879), chief architect of the company. Their idyllic or romantically-heroic
stories are told in a unique choreographic style which makes a novel
theatrical experience.

Nowhere else has theatre-dancing been so consistently used to create an
entertainment in exquisite visual taste, whose impact is predominantly a
lovely excitement rather than a dramatic adventure.

In turn both Fokine and Balanchine were guest-choreographers in
Copenhagen in the 1920s and 1930s. In recent years many modern re-
productions of existing ballets have been made by Scandinavian, English
and American choreographers. All these 20th-century works exist to
provide a wider repertory and to enlarge the dancers' talents in utilising
a fresh manner of projection.

Now, although the festival leans heavily on the reputation of Bournonville and his works, most of them have been banished from its
programmes. Only *La Sylphide* and one act of his long ballet *Napoli*
(together with the perennial *Giselle*) were shown this year. Some of the
thirteen modern ballets shown were not good enough as festival-pieces.

This unbalance arises from simple causes. The Danish training method
is blended with a performing style proper to Bournonville's works. But
this style is not fluid enough to enable performers to give the highest
theatrical expression to modern choreography, which uses a good deal of
the common vocabulary of 19th-century European classicism and also,
at times, demands facility in the neo-classicism which has been expanding
everywhere, save in Denmark, since the 1920s.

27 May, 1961.

The most original Scandinavian post-war talent is that of Birgit Cullberg, the Swedish choreographer of *Miss Julie,* a paraphrase of Strindberg's play, and *The Moon Reindeer,* a Lapp legend of the same epic simplicity as that behind the structure of *Swan Lake.*

Her choreography, firm in outline, forcefully dramatic and using a close-grained classical vocabulary, partly derives from her study with her greatest mentor, Kurt Jooss.

*Miss Julie* drags out its one-act play length to an hour's worth of passion, nastiness and peasant rawness—almost but not quite dulling the edge of its ruthless drama.

*The Moon Reindeer,* a tale of blood, possession and death, has a special eerie beauty helpfully contributed to by Riisager's forceful neo-Sibelian score and by Per Falk's glittering décor of lighting and highly inventive projections. In both these, the heroine was danced by Mona Vangsaa with a whole and fine-cut characterisation.

The native dance talent is such that performance *can* embrace a wider style; unfortunately, as this festival has shown, the style begins to slip almost as soon as the visiting choreographer has left Copenhagen.

Some of the good modern works are being heavily misinterpreted and much good production and talent is thrown into foreign-made ballets of no great quality.

29 May, 1961.

This second point was illustrated with crushing emphasis in Roland Petit's version of *Cyrano de Bergerac,* shown in London two years ago and recently staged by him here.

For a still young artist Henning Kronstam brings some powerfully precise acting to the leading role. As against Petit's own interpretation in Paris and London, Kronstam makes Cyrano more civilised and less bombastic; he is much more a worldly-wise man resigned to his ludicrous deformity. This interpretation sets the key to which the production is geared. Every role is performed with studied care and in mosaically minute detail. All of this merely emphasises the choreographic poverty of most of the work and leaves an impression of a vast expenditure of time, talent and energy on something theatrically almost meaningless. The characterisation of Cyrano is simply impossible without the medium of words.

Another aspect of this odd treatment of modern works is shown in the newest version of *Apollon Musagète,* which Balanchine staged here in 1957, completely re-creating the original Diaghilev ballet of 1928.

The importance of this work has always lain in its alliance of a perfectly simple balletic theme with a fresh ingenuity of neo-classic dance forms, the whole tightly embraced in and illuminated by one of Stravinsky's best-ever dance scores. A stark setting and minimal costuming allows full freedom of dancing and acting. We see the young Apollo being born, realising his own gifts, then conferring their talents upon Polyhymnia, Terpsichore and Calliope; each and all celebrating the magic of art through highly original dances in solo and concert.

Now, possibly subconsciously infected by the all-too-human view of Greek mythology propagated by Thorwaldsen, the local sculptor, the dancers act and smile and play to the audience when they should remain detached, lovely and untouchable.

The choreography is still miraculous, but half its impact is thrown away by the obviousness of the dancing and the ruthlessness to which Stravinsky's tempos are subjected.

27 May, 1961.

As a sort of counterblast to all these modernisms Erik Bruhn, the company's leading male dancer, partnering Kirsten Simone, appeared in that old-fashioned firework display, the Pas de Deux from *Don Quixote*. He effortlessly lifted it out of the category of technical showpiece to the level of a dance ecstasy such as we really rarely witness nowadays, something not very far away from what Nijinsky must have been able to do.

He was the embodiment of nobility, vigour and elegance. Nobody else dancing can achieve quite this, and as his present form excels anything I have seen in him before, his dancing is already marked as one of the glories of this year's ballet, and not only in Copenhagen.

3 June, 1961.

So Danish ballet stands today at a cross-roads, and must quickly decide its new direction. National sentiment and the sense of heritage, which all the dancers acquire during their training, tend towards upholding the unique national repertoire.

Yet the company's recently won international reputation also demands that it shall accept the challenge of comparison with the big internationally-performing companies of France, Britain and America.

This is no impossibility provided the training system maintains the spirit of the Bournonville style and at the same time enables its dancers to acquire that further flexibility which will equip them to do justice to more modern, more exotic choreographic methods.

## THE DANISH BALLET AND MUSIC FESTIVAL (1966)

From *The Daily Telegraph*, 26 May, 1966.

For an annual artistic occasion with 17 years continuity, the Danish Ballet and Music Festival is in better health all round than it has been for the past decade. The crop of young talents which the ballet school has turned out since 1960 includes many people of extraordinary ability and with well-integrated performing craft.

Additionally, the works shown in the festival are, with few exceptions, in mint condition as productions and their casts dance as though the honour of Denmark as well as of their own careers depended on the good impressions they make.

No other company anywhere presents Lichine's *Graduation Ball*, now 25 years old, with quite the Copenhagen level of brilliant dancing and effervescent atmosphere.

The work is a cleverly nostalgic picture of the romantic Vienna of pre-1914 days, set in an aristocratic finishing school for young ladies who entertain the students of a neighbouring military academy for an end-of-term ball.

Lichine's workmanlike choreography and Dorati's clean-cut arrangements of Johann Strauss music work smoothly together. And in an oddly inspired fashion the Danish temperament draws out exactly the perfect qualities for the interpretation of these touching boy-meets-girl situations.

The hesitations of youth, the boldness of first flirtations are presented with great finesse of detail and there is not one iota of false sentiment anywhere.

Amongst numerous complete characterisations the most notable were those of Fredbjørn Bjørnsson as the General, Inge Sand as the Principal of the Ladies' Academy, Niels Kehlet as the Drummer Boy and Dinna Bjørn as the tomboy who nearly wrecks the romantic atmosphere for her senior colleagues.

From *The Daily Telegraph*, 23 May, 1966.

Last Wednesday saw the final performance before retirement of Margrethe Schanne, the company's romantic ballerina, in *La Sylphide*. It was an occasion which clearly marked the end of that era in which this festival was founded and acquired world fame.

Yet the two following performances, displaying Anna Laerkesen in *Night Shadow* and *The Moon Reindeer* were just as obviously the opening of a fresh period which will be historically distinguished by the interpretations of her splendid talent.

This is a dancer destined for greatness and her performances are illuminated by that ease of execution and total depth of characterisation which only a handful of ballerinas have commanded in the past hundred years.

Other pleasures were performances in familiar roles by guest artists Toni Lander and Erik Bruhn, in *The Conservatoire, Don Quixote* and *Miss Julie.*

Another benefit is the recent appointment after wide experience in France and America of the younger choreographer Flemming Flindt as artistic director.

It is his new production of *The Three Musketeers*—fast, furious and frenetic—among a group of ballets half classic, half contemporary, which is the spectacular focal point of the festival. However, as with many attempts to translate novels and plays into ballets, this one mingles eye-catching episodes of splendid drama or startling beauty with long passages of overweighted and repetitive dances, miming, posturing and violent slapstick.

## THE ROYAL DANISH BALLET, COPENHAGEN (October, 1966)

From *The Daily Telegraph*, 31 October, 1966.

Careful reconstitution of the unique Bournonville ballets of a century ago is part of a process by the Royal Danish Ballet to create a wide focus and popular image for ballet in Copenhagen.

*Kermesse in Bruges,* unperformed for nearly a decade, has been rebuilt at the Royal Theatre from the original architectural plan by its artistic director Flemming Flindt and its ex-dancer Hans Brenaa and was staged last week.

Created in 1851, it is probably the only surviving comic ballet a century old. Its mixture of comedy of situation, action-comedy and charming sentiment provides eighty minutes' worth of lively entertainment.

Its story is loosely based on a medieval Flemish legend and concerns the adventures of three brothers of Bruges who go adventuring assisted by magic gifts of a ring, a sword and a violin. Their difficulties are mostly amatory ones and a persistent note of happy romantic recklessness colours every situation.

The plot, with its hints of rebellion against social and religious convention, its tribute to the adventurousness of happy youth and its gentle but constant mocking of authority, gives *Kermesse in Bruges* its unique place among surviving 19th century ballets.

This keenly imagined production retains all the original choreography, adds some modest solo dances for the brothers and sets the action in three continuous scenes to provide a non-stop spectacle.

The "period décor" of Jacques Nöel rather follows the convention of Bournonville's own time but with a nicely contrived and controlled opulence that happily fits the story's atmosphere. The well-designed costumes use strong colour and ingenious pattern so that they carry the correct medieval look, yet are light and sensible for dancing in.

The middle scene, in which as though by means of a truly Copernican telescope the brothers' fiancées see them afar off dallying in exotic female company, is a splendid theatrical tour de force.

Balletically the main fascination of the work lies in Bournonville's rich variety of expressive dances for both male and female created out of a simple but refined step vocabulary.

Ensembles include religious processions, carnival scenes and kermesse dances and duels artfully spectacular but without any overloading of detail. The score by H. S. Paulli lacks the dramatic imagery of an Adolphe Adam but in its lightweight melodic structure is perfectly fitted to its choreographic task.

The ballet provides a big handful of full-dimensional roles and many vivid character-sketches among the supporters.


## THE STUTTGART FESTIVALS OF 1965 AND 1967, AND THE CHOREOGRAPHY OF JOHN CRANKO

Compiled from notices in *The Daily Telegraph*.

From *The Daily Telegraph*, 1 June, 1965.

Few of Europe's ballet festivals can be so firmly based on the work of one man as the one in Stuttgart, where John Cranko, formerly of the Royal Ballet, is artistic director and chief choreographer.

His most recent group of works include many stamped with the signature that he impressed on his early ballets in London. His main qualification is as a producer of movement; his choreography, always interesting if at times undisciplined, shows that his imagination runs ahead of his invention. Yet this is an advantage when working with this Stuttgart company of many nationalities and mixed talents.

His recent creation of *Romeo and Juliet* to the Prokofiev score is as notable a work as the other contemporary, more widely known, versions of Lavrovsky, Ashton and MacMillan. The story unfolds with equal emphasis on the pageantry, the ensembles, the clever secondary characterisations, a totally extrovert Romeo and a splendidly lyrical Juliet.

The fine organisation of entries, groups, choreographic dialogue and solo dances combines with the frequently beautiful but sometimes erratic sets and costumes of Jurgen Rose to impress upon the ballet an appropriate Italo-German quality.

This is Renaissance Italy boldly interpreted in Germanic terms; magnificent, romantic, heroic and not overweighted with sentimentality and pomp—almost as though the original text were the work not of Shakespeare but of some German romantic poet.

Carla Fracci, a guest artist from Milan, made Juliet a passionate and compassionate child of her times as she assumed and developed Cranko's choreographic vision effortlessly.

Her opulent yet sensitive acting and dancing blended to produce one of the most lyrically touching interpretations among all modern ballet's Juliets. This was a theatrical creation packed with that total Italian commitment that would have won praise from Stendhal.

Her Romeo, Ray Barra, a turbulent dynamo of extrovert dancing and acting, seemed to belong to some other nation, even some other century, than did Juliet.

From *The Daily Telegraph*, 3 June, 1965.

*Swan Lake* follows the commonly used four-act pattern, most of the original's choreography being present in acts two and four. The remainder is largely freshly-devised by Mr Cranko. Jurgen Rose's décor confers appropriate alternations of Teutonic mistiness and exuberant fancy on the action.

Birgit Keil, a local talent, English-trained, gave Odette-Odile a complete if rather tightly compressed character. Richard Cragun, from California, also London-schooled, was a strong and convincing Prince Siegfried. Opulent spectacle, a mass of fascinating minor-key characters and lively dancing provided what this newly-awakened local ballet company wants.

No masterpiece of European literature is less promising as a ballet scenario than Pushkin's *Eugene Onegin*; its unique moods and atmosphere, its subtle characters and its very unheroic hero are not the stuff of which theatre is made.

The ballet was a bold, not foolish, attempt to create a romantic-dramatic study of character; but Pushkin's agile, suave and sympathetic imaginings cannot be expressed and illuminated through silent dance, mime and action.

Onegin's honesty and arrogance, which lead to the ruin of three other lives as well as his own, are revealed in Pushkin's great statement about honesty and the glory of the human spirit.

The ballet turns out to be a neat melodrama and the fates of the leading quartet are worked out, too simply, for what appeared to be the mechanical accidents of Lenski's death, Olga's heartbreak, Tatiana's defensive tactics and Onegin's stubbornness.

Where Pushkin loaded the poem with marvellous observations of mood and motive, dominated by an ironic affection for the characters, the ballet is an episode of romantic misunderstandings.

Yet the four principals had clear notions of the essence of the matter. They gave their characters firmly correct outlines but could not fill in the all-too-human details, which is essential.

Marcia Haydée, a Brazilian, as Tatiana, Ray Barra, an American, as Onegin, Egon Madsen, a Dane, as Lenski and Ana Cardus, a Mexican, as Olga, worked marvellously together and gave to this odd experiment all the virtue it had.

## 1967

From *The Daily Telegraph*, 12 May, 1967.

Possibly Mr Cranko's boldest experiment with a big scale non-narrative ballet is *L'Estro Armonico*, thirty minutes of dance patterns in exciting variety and configuration based on three linked concertos of Vivaldi.

Mr Cranko's skill here is to create original groupings whose strong lyrical overtones gloriously illuminate the delight and the dignity that the opposing sexes find in their dancing together.

Ana Cardus, a ballerina of minute stature and superbly delicate qualities, unselfconsciously dominated the action throughout. Maximo Molina, another London-trained dancer, showed himself a strong and attractive partner in these ingenious commentaries on Vivaldi's music.

From *The Daily Telegraph*, 15 May, 1967.

Cranko's best comic work, *Jeu de Cartes*, was performed with every broad stroke of caricature and every feathery touch of irony perfectly accented.

The choreography of this larger-than-life poker game complements Stravinsky's glittering score. Together, dancing and music provide an amusingly mordant commentary on naïveté, folly and pretentiousness. The work is a particularly stringent test of male dancing and Cranko's grotesque inventions were boldly performed by a well-unified male ensemble.

Alan Beale's designing was seen in Cranko's new work, *Quatre Images,* a ballet using four Ravel episodes as framework for a story of princely amours and bewitchment, with a romantically melancholy ending. Though showing phases of nice dance invention here and there the choreography did not unify all the elements of the plot and never developed the kind of inevitability that such a story demands.

The Cranko touch was much clearer and very effective in a group of divertissements. One, to Grieg music, displayed the elegant vivacity of Birgit Keil and Heinz Clauss, two German dancers coming to strong maturity in this company.

*La Source* was a re-make of a tender romantic pas de deux on Delibes music, with Ana Cardus, a deliciously nymph-like heroine, and Richard Cragun, a bold hero.

*Hommage à la Bolshoi,* to some opulent music of Glazunov, is a balletic "in joke", suggesting that what the Russians can do superbly can perhaps be successfully imitated by dancers of a different school. It enabled Marcia Haydée and (again) Mr Cragun to disport themselves boldly in strong acrobatic dancing that yet had a velvet smooth finish.

From *The Daily Telegraph,* 13 May, 1967.
The Stuttgart Ballet Company's wide repertoire includes several big-scale ballets, both originals and revivals, none of which is so untraditional as Cranko's newest, a remaking of *The Nutcracker.*

In this version the original plot of a child's fairy tale is re-worked into a fantasy story of teenagers in love. Its leading characters are the flirtatious Lene and her soldier-boy-friend Konrad. Artfully retaining most of the episodes and characters of the original, Mr Cranko has made an action-ballet in the plot of which there is a heavy undercurrent of the sinister. This particular Christmas party involves Lene's rivals in Konrad's affections; the air, metaphorically, and the décor, literally, are heavy with hints of that cruelty and ruthlessness that lie behind so many fairy tales.

Mr Cranko's choreography unfolds in a steady flow of dance inventions, some prettily effective, a few confused, but most of them illustrating his daring reassessment of the plot, even if it is not to all ballet-goers' tastes.

Ralph Adron's sets and costumes mingle a pretty pictorialism with some fairly ominous fetishist symbols. The dominant character is Konrad, here given a splendid performance by Egon Madsen, who danced and acted with notable style and grace.

To provide ninety per cent of repertoire of such wide-ranging types of ballet confirms Cranko's stature as one of the most imaginative young directors of a European company today.


NEW YORK (1949 and 1950)

1949

From *Ballet and Opera*, March, 1949.

Very few dancers, and even fewer ballets, of American origin have been seen in England since the beginning of this century's renaissance. To enjoy fully all that can be seen in today's American dance-theatres, the European spectator must put aside his home-made impressions of the American dance and dancers seen on London or Paris stages in recent years. Despite its alleged internationalism (the only true international aspect of ballet is its Form—never its Content), ballet, whether practised in American, English, French, Italian or Soviet Russian theatres, is best experienced inside its own *milieu*. If one cannot see a ballet company on its native ground—where one will inevitably have had to make some readjustment to strange theatres and even stranger audiences—one must project oneself into a frame of mind closely akin to that of its own audience if one is seeing it away from its usual surroundings. All the foregoing is perhaps an obvious exposition of the fact that few of us have real affinity with the cultural atmosphere of any country or society other than our own: yet probably half the failures amongst all kinds of theatre works shown to foreign audiences are due to the neglect of this hard fact by the impresarios concerned.

This observation was prompted by my first experience of a theatre-dance performance in America, at which I saw Paul Draper on my second day in New York. Draper has had extensive training in tap, ballet and modern and has devised a choreographic, and a dancing, style which make use of all three techniques. The theatre was packed for a Sunday matinee; no programme was available, and Mr Draper apologised for this lack, which was due to his confusing two performances; he would act as *compère* and announce the items. He used two pianists, singly and in duet, and for some items they were reinforced by a skilful exponent with the percussion battery normally found in a hot dance-band. Draper danced to Schubert, Handel, Bach, Strauss and folk-song music; he announced each item in a pleasantly informal style, taking the audience into his confidence, talking about previous performances, adding such intimate observations as: 'This is a number I normally do in expensive night-clubs; it costs more to see it there than you paid today.' He has excellent stage sense and never overstrains for effect, yet everything is neatly danced and beautifully finished; his style looks like the perfect screen-dance formula, and it is easy to see why he has such success in the night-club and Hollywood *milieux.* Some items were given without music, including a study of an electioneering politician addressing an audience wherein the mime and gesture were as vivid and comprehensible as anything to be seen, I dare say, on any European stage. The audience was electric, hanging on every word, gesture and step, detonating its applause on the split-second each number ended, and chattering madly between items. The native passion—and it really is a passion in its intensity—for something virile, athletic and graceful was well demonstrated on this occasion . . . The passion can sometimes spill over in an exuberance of spontaneity during what (to unaccustomed ears) seem the wrong moments—as when, for example, the greater part of the 3,000-odd audience at City Center on 13 January clapped every entrance and every feat of execution by each of the five principal dancers in the opening ballet. Even in the last ballet at the tenth of a ten-performance season, I found it hard to forgive my neighbours' uninhibited reaction when applause burst into the midst of sustained orchestral passages in such works as *Symphony in C* (Bizet), *Divertimento* (Haieff), and *Symphonie Concertante* (Mozart); yet this spontaneity is the important clue to understanding what American audiences want of their dancers. If what is seen touches either heart or mind (both of which organs seem to function with hair-trigger delicacy amongst New York audiences), together come two or three thousand pairs of palms in a fusillade which completely blots out the orchestra for several seconds. Of course this audience had something to clap about, by any standards. The season was the second given this winter at City Center by the New York City Ballet: the Press for the October season was magnificently generous—and was written by a group of critics whose collective sympathy with, and comprehension of ballet, is serious, sensible and concise.

Ballet Society, organised by Lincoln Kirstein in 1946, was a private subscription club, promoting occasional shows of ballet on the highest professional standards. City Center is a theatre with a stage not larger than that of Sadler's Wells, in a house seating about 3,500; the building is city property and can be leased tax-free for ballet, opera or plays, provided top price does not exceed three dollars. As any Broadway success charges six dollars for the West-End equivalent of a 12s. 6d. stall, City Center inhibits all managements save those who can put on a worthy spectacle which can just cover expenses when playing to good business. Hence Ballet Society was reborn as New York City Ballet, and this recent season has been a testing of the New York audience's supporting strength; for, by showing that there existed a *need* for good ballet this company has won the concession of being the resident ballet company of New York. Henceforth this company shares City Center with the New York Opera and the New York Orchestra: this trinity of projects housed in this theatre is roughly the cultural and organisational equivalent of the Old Vic and Sadler's Wells Theatres during the 1930s.

The repertoire for the season consisted of: *Four Temperaments* (Hindemith); *Symphony in C* (Bizet); *Divertimento* (Haieff); *Symphonie Concertante* (Mozart); *Concerto Barocco* (Bach); *Orpheus* (Stravinsky); and *Serenade* (Tchaikovsky)—all by Balanchine. Tudor's *Time Table* (music, Copland: scenery and costumes, Morcom) was given its first U.S. performance, having been seen originally only on a South American tour in 1941. Jerome Robbins' *The Guests* (music, Marc Blitzstein) was presented on 20 January. Merce Cunningham's *The Seasons* (music, John Cage: scenery and costumes, Isamu Noguchi) and Bolender's *Mother Goose Suite* (to the Ravel music) completed the repertoire.

Balanchine has been director of the School of American Ballet (founded 1934) and chief choreographer to Ballet Society since the inception of both organisations, and because his position as the most important living choreographer is recognised by critics and audience alike in New York, the large number of his works in this repertoire is understandable and, further, is the safest financial guarantee the company has for its seasons. It is not possible to analyse and evaluate Balanchine's style in this limited space: very little of his output since 1933 has been seen in Europe, and it is during the fourteen years spent in America that his classical style has completely matured, and even extended. The seven of his works shown in this season reveal a richness of dance-and-movement invention such as I suggest the Western theatre has never before known: Fokine may have invented more diverse forms of *dance-acting,* and Massine has achieved both a greater number of intense *dramatic moments,* and of pyrotechnical ensembles, than Balanchine shows. Only Balanchine—within my experience—has extended and amplified the pure classicism bred out of Perrot and Taglioni via Petipa and Ivanov, and has, further, simplified and heightened the intensity of lyric and tragic movement (*not* dancing) to a point not to be seen in the surviving works of all the choreographers since Viganò.

*Concerto Barocco* and *Le Palais de Cristal* (first version of the Bizet symphony) are known to a small proportion of European audiences: these two works plus *Symphonie Concertante* and *Divertimento* are purely dancing ballets, yet as individual, as varied in their richnesses, and as serenely classical as are so many Bach fugues or Mozart symphonies.

## 1950
From *Ballet*, September/October, 1950.
*Concerto Barocco* to music of Bach, in décor and costumes of Eugene Berman, presents a rarified style of dance imagery closely moulded (but not tightly integrated in bar-for-step fashion) to the majestic, sonorous and unstrained musical background of Bach's Double-Violin Concerto. It is one of Balanchine's strongest statements of the fact that a ballet is a spectacle of dancing, and any illumination of character or suggestion of personality comes only incidentally from the dancer's manner of demonstrating that he—or she—is primarily, in this context of Time and Space, a creator of fascinating pattern of movement. The solo instruments are echoed by two *danseuses* who are given background, contrast and amplification of their dance-figures by a *corps de ballet* of eight girls; a male soloist appears for part of the ballet, to provide mechanical aid to the females' dance images and to create—for part of the action only—a strong undertone of masculine dancing which stresses the extended lyricism of the two female dancers. The pattern of action unfolds in figures of dance for one or other soloist, or both together, counterpointed against the harder, more obvious, heavily scored patterns which the *corps de ballet* create.

*Serenade* is a wonderful danced episode with added lyrical overtones which grow out of a hinted-at, half-suggested, unstressed emotional complex between two female characters and one male. *Four Temperaments* falls somewhat below the usual Balanchine standard of choreography; it adheres too closely to the music, and although the dance-patterns are as ingenious as the Seligman costumes, I never felt that it differentiated the four temperaments (melancholic, sanguine, phlegmatic and choleric) sufficiently theatrically. This was an occasion on which one could say that a Homer in our midst had nodded.

*Orpheus* is the most recent treatment of this myth from Balanchine's hand; more than one earlier version to the Gluck music was made by him. Here the score was written by Stravinsky in full collaboration with the choreographer, the plot incidents being fully worked out before a single note was committed to paper; and Isamu Noguchi's lengthy experience as a designer of abstract and fantastic costumes and properties seems to me to have reached its culmination in his simple and serenely awe-full masks, garments, lyres, branches and architectural pieces. The Time is eternity and the Place is everywhere that Man inhabits, in this dreadful and simple statement of the classic myth; sometimes the movement is so simple that only the most exquisite performers can keep the shape of the incidents inside the frameworks of both the music and the stage-space. More than one critic has acclaimed it as the outstanding theatrical achievement of the past decade, and I place it amongst the three most memorable works seen in a quarter-of-a-century's balletgoing.

Tudor's *Time Table* is woven round the comings-and-goings of people at a small railroad station about the year 1917; girls waiting for their soldier-lovers, marines flirting with a party of teenagers, a newspaper reader, a station-master. Neither subject nor the plot permits as emphatic a pattern of behaviour as it to be found in the earlier *Jardin aux Lilas,* or the later *Pillar of Fire.* As the various lovers are parted, maybe for ever, one returning warrior steps off the train to be greeted by a girl who has waited throughout the 'story' in the background; a tender touch which throws all the preceding incidents into clear focus as the curtain falls. Set and costumes were over-realistic, while Copland's score was clear, agreeable for dancing and lacking in 'effects' or obvious mannerisms.

Bolender's *Mother Goose Suite* is strictly apprentice-choreography but simple and effective in its adherence to the music—rather than in any marked affinity with the fantasy suggested by the 'story'; the unacknowledged costumes were deplorably unsuitable to either the music or the fantasy incidents which formed the basis of the plot.

Merce Cunningham's *The Seasons* is an oddity, choreographed in what seems strict adherence to the tenets of 'Modern Dance'; in a limited vocabulary of movement and with too many repetitions of esoteric entries and exits. John Cage's score is, however, exciting music of the 'anti-French' modernistic school; Isamu Noguchi designed the unusual costumes and symbolic objects which the dancers carried, wore or moved around the stage at several points.

Jerome Robbins has made few ballets in the past three years, and his return from 'Broadway choreography' was a welcome event. *The Guests* is dramatically very potent but choreographically rather a routine affair—less exciting than *Interplay* but tighter in structure and clearer emotionally than his *Fancy Free,* both works known to London audiences. A master of ceremonies greets an assembly of guests, a group of whom wear a species of caste-mark on their foreheads; the unmarked ones refuse to mingle with them, and each group dances its rather obviously geometric patterns alone. Then a boy from one group meets a girl from the other, and they perform a marvellous kind of ritual dance of love-and-despair, ignored by both groups. When they discover their caste differences they try to rejoin their own parties, but both are spurned and cast into outer darkness by their former colleagues. The costumes ('abstract' in design) in flame, black and mauve, and black-and-lilac panelled backcloth made a strikingly eerie setting and frame for the proceedings. Blitzstein's score was too close to a conscious cleverness to be wholly satisfying as dance-music; but this was an occasion on which most of the audience lapped up the 'social significance' aspect of the work and tossed balletic values into the same outer darkness which swallowed the unfortunate lovers.

Nearly all the dancers in this company are products of the School of American Ballet, which is, in effect, Balanchine's Academy. Maria Tallchief, Tanaquil LeClercq, Marie-Jeanne and Beatrice Tomkins are both exciting dancers and vivid personalities; the male contingent led by Magallanes, Moncion, Bolender, Bliss and Beard offers them worthy support. Academically, they are finely equipped but variable in their degrees of stage experience; Tallchief and Marie-Jeanne are completely bred and fully trained ballerinas whose brilliance overshadows the remainder of the company . . . and one asks oneself what standards of execution and projection were presented by any company seen previously before it had completed its first thirty public performances?


## THE NEW YORK CITY BALLET IN NEW YORK (1962)

From *Dance and Dancers*, April, 1962.

Twenty-five days is, of course, too little and too much; too little time for seeing all the interesting things happening in the theatres of several cities—too much if you have to keep going at a lively pace, mostly living out of a suitcase, and rising too many mornings at 6.30 to catch a plane to somewhere else.

But in twenty-five days I fitted in twenty-three performances, watched classes and rehearsals, had (seemingly) hundreds of hours' discussion with dancers, choreographers, impresarios of every age, style and temper. Between these things I flew about 3,000 miles from city to city, saw films and art galleries, and contrived to avoid nervous fatigue in New York and frostbite in Winnipeg (I even ate sometimes and, occasionally, slept).

The first six friends I met in New York said either, "Why weren't you here last week? You have missed So-and-So", or they said, "Pity you can't stay another week, you could have seen Such-and-Such". Well, I didn't see anything of Martha Graham or Company, but I watched two Modern companies new to me; I saw enough of their work to measure fairly accurately the aims and achievements of the New York City Ballet and, elsewhere, those of Illinois, Canadian National and Royal Winnipeg Ballets; enough musicals to catch on to present trends in good musical-choreography. Without doubt, I saw some of the most invigorating male dancing on view anywhere today, and I got some of the finest playing of ballet music that can be heard anywhere—from New York City Ballet's orchestra under Robert Irving.

It is almost ten years since New York's company was in London, and the differences since then, though many, have not altered the essential quality of the company. There is still the same firm core of leading dancers at the top: Diana Adams, Melissa Hayden, Patricia Wilde, with Todd Bolender, Francisco Moncion, Nicholas Magallanes, with some stunning additions, notably Violette Verdy, now more than a passing "guest", Allegra Kent, Jacques d'Amboise and Conrad Ludlow. There is a whole fresh crop (indeed, there have been several such crops in the decade) of young dancers, now including Suki Schorer, Gloria Govrin, Carol Sumner and Patricia Neary.

Since its London visit, the company has staged about twenty-four ballets by Balanchine and seven or eight by others. Many of these are out of the current repertoire, some of them possibly until such time as Balanchine feels it desirable to revive them on particular dancer-talents. This extraordinary rate of turnover of ballets is one of the most individual features of this company. It derives mainly from Balanchine's simple but unanswerable argument, that as new dancers are continuously being fed from the school into the company, so new ballets must be made—partly to exploit their individual talents, and partly because Balanchine cannot continue as director-choreographer-teacher unless he can regularly test his own invention, his musical sensibility and his belief in his dancers by creating more and more new ballets. This world-shaking formula might be applied with advantage to a few of the world's older ballet companies. Certainly here it produces a repertoire which, though largely consisting of Balanchine ballets, is full of infinite varieties of subtle (but perfectly comprehensible) choreography.

Since he began his career in America, less than thirty years ago, Balanchine has made over seventy ballets and choreographed about two dozen musicals and films. Most ballets seem to last about two years, except for the continuously popular successes which appear season after season: and if he were asked, Balanchine could make a convincing case for scrapping a ballet once it has served to advance the talent or capacity of even only one budding soloist. Such a dancer, though she may appear in fewer performances a year than her counterpart in London, Paris or

Copenhagen, will have regularly six, seven or eight interesting rôles for at least a year or more.

Of the ten ballets in this season new to me, none could be faulted for seeming repetitive or for surface similarities to earlier works I knew. This is simply because—as has been often noted before, and by a wide range of commentators—his invention with both the existing basic classic vocabulary and with his own developments and permutations on it enable him to create movement-patterns which unfailingly grip the attention of an eye attuned to fascinating movement.

The ballets unknown here which I saw included the new full-length *Midsummer Night's Dream,* which is largely interesting because its first act delineates almost perfectly successfully Shakespeare's tangled story in a fluid kind of dance and dance-plus-naturalistic-mime; this is a choreographic mode which Balanchine has rarely used. The second act is a *Grand Divertissement* which excuses bringing in just about every member of the cast; a series of occasionally over-complex *ballabiles* framing some firmly "classic" *pas de deux* and solos.

*Agon* is probably the most difficult ballet yet achieved, to demonstrate what depths of subtlety and waves of nuance its creator can apply to, and draw out of, the music and the actual dance-personalities of its performers. Stravinsky's score is about the limit that he can reach in pure tonal and rhythmic refinement; and Balanchine can be seen to have accepted an unspoken challenge in fitting it to a scheme of dance-movement which is worth performing *only* because it enables (compels, even) each dancer to refine to the ultimate every personal quirk of stance, leap, elevation, gesture, posture, that he or she has developed as personal style. Watching Verdy, Kent, Sumner and Neary in partnership and in opposition with Mitchell, Villella, Watts and Rapp (plus four other girls—a minor *corps de ballet*), you see flashing out of the movement more and more subtle "tones" or body-expressions than you have noted in everything they have danced before. Above all ballets I have ever seen, this one takes more from you and gives more back than any other composed piece of regulated movement. In balance against the rest of the repertoire, it should probably be given only four or five times a season, and it has to be seen this number of times, I feel sure, to permit the spectator to grasp just how rewarding its celestial marriage of music and movement is.

*Liebeslieder Walzer* exists at just about the opposite pole; two sets of Brahms' Waltzes (Op. 52 and 65) are played fourhands by pianists Louise Sherman and Robert Irving with a vocal quartet grouped at the piano on stage; these six are "period-dressed" like the octet of dancers. The first series of pieces frame a ballroom episode wherein the dancing is wholly social in character—as though we were looking through a missing fourth wall at a private ball in the 1820s. There are clever accelerations of pace and passion and the curtain suddenly falls. It rises quickly to show a fantasy décor superimposed on the formal ballroom with a starry, blue sky overhead and the female dancers now in balleticised versions of their former dress. The whole quality of the dances is transmuted into smooth balletic form (though each dance remains sweetly geared to its waltz rhythm). The eight young folk have moved out of their romantic dream into a world of romance, and concoct for us an endlessly developing group of balletic figurings all choreographically related to the earlier, formal dances. But the whole adventure is an exposition of dance-mood; as indescribable in its varieties of impact (or the manner of that impact) as is *Agon*.

*Valses et Variations* was the first novelty of this season and was nicely "run in" by the time I came to it. Set to a dozen-odd pieces from Glazounov's *Raymonda* score, it is essence-of-Petipa refined into the new essence-of-Balanchine. If Balanchine had worked directly under the old master, one feels that this is exactly the ballet he could have made under firm instructions about duration and accenting. Yet the dances have a three-dimensionalism that is lacking in, for instance, the opulent variations in *The Sleeping Beauty* or the current Soviet version of *Raymonda*. This dancing has a wider range of ocular (as distinct from image-invoking) appeal, simply because Balanchine has worked out, more exactly than any 19th century choreographer ever had to, the possibilities of displaying more of the body's facets in continuous movement. Apart from the unapologetic exhibitionism of the leading rôles (Patricia Wilde and Jacques d'Amboise) there are individual variations for each of five soloists—five "fairies" to measure against the "six good fairies" of *The Sleeping Beauty* prologue.

*Allegro Brillante* (1956) is reported to have been described by its creator as "everything I know about classical ballet in thirteen minutes"! It soars away from, rather than leans against, the single complete movement of Tchaikovsky's unfinished (and insipid) Third Piano Concerto. Charming lyricism is its keynote, and its unique signature is a vast richness of wide-spaced movement, with big, well-accented arm gestures—as though the concentrated floor-space used were being deliberately balanced by a more than usually inventive use of the dancers' air-surround.

*Ivesiana* (music of Charles Ives—a "Saturday" composer) is a Balanchine shocker, in as much as it is stylistically quite unlike any of the regular neo-classical works. It is a moody romantic piece expressing dream-ideas keyed to some amazing music, as individual as Stravinsky's, with such titles as

"Central Park in the Dark", "The Unanswered Question", "In the Inn and in the Night". Then there were *Stars and Stripes* and *Western Symphony*, both bright, breezy (and partly purely corny) examples of Americana. The first is in deliberately faked-up but very dashing Civil War period military costumes, and is done to Hershy Kay's neat pastiches of Sousa's military music. *Western Symphony*, again to Kay music, blends folksy-type airs and dance idiom but enfolds the latter in a flexible framework of classical spacings, formulas and gestural patterns.

*Symphony in C* was very thinly danced when I saw it; *La Sonnambula* (in Europe, *Night Shadow*) showed the splendid Allegra Kent in the title rôle, and Anthony Blunt took the roof off with the dynamic comedy of his Harlequin dance. *Apollo* had one of its (usual) fine performances with Conrad Ludlow giving a glowing, youthful accent to the hero and supported by a trio of goddesses (Kent, Wilde and Jillana) who were deliciously varied in personality and style, so as to effectively create again the awesome vernal freshness of the legend.

Jerome Robbins's four works were not shown very impressively; *Interplay* and *Fanfare* seemed to be done as private jokes for their casts. *Afternoon of a Faun,* with Patricia McBride and Edward Villella, is less explosive than the "Ballets: USA" version seen here, but *feels* psychologically more plausible. *The Cage* was notable, primarily, for displaying McBride's rich talent as the Novice; she was pathetically effective as a believable half-animal, half-human creature.

If a lot of the foregoing suggests that I almost unconditionally enjoyed the New York City Ballet repertoire—well, I did! Long before I thought of it, someone else said that Balanchine is a "very Mozart of choreographers". He *is* a Mozart, in that most of his dance-images are pure and emotionally unreferential; they have seemingly "natural" shape and rhythmic texture and also clear harmonic originality. He can also be compared, not exaggeratedly, to a Tchaikovsky for the high-strained yet unhysterical romanticism of his more "humane" episodes—even to a Stravinsky, for he has shown in many works that he can match, subtly underscore and even add overtones (visually) to that master's ballet scores. As with Mozart, one can, of course, tire of an endless diet; but to taste again, after an empty decade, a round dozen of his ballets, is to suffer a sharp shock to one's current notions of what are the acceptable limits of 20th century choreography. A three-piece programme of his ballets shows more actual created choreography than most Westerners have achieved in a lifetime of ballet-making. Two further points: this sort of dance-invention, released and revealed through his sort of high-bred dancers, would simply not be possible without the consistently high level of orchestral music that he requires, and makes sure of getting. And: one can therefore to an extent sympathise with those American critics and regular ballet-goers who claim that Balanchine consistently over-emphasises what is, after all, only one element in the classic structure of 20th century ballet, viz., its musical accompaniment. He is often well content with the notion that the music suggests certain possible co-ordinations of a group of bodies in new patterns, with fresh accents of gesture, unique floor-patterns and time-durations; and that traditional décor and elaborate dresses and any hint of story or event or characterisation are so many cluttering nuisances!


## BALLET IN AMERICA (1966)

From *The Daily Telegraph,* 13 April, 1966

In one sweeping generalisation, ballet in America today is more exciting to watch than here because choreographers choose more daring themes and much more daring music, and have dancers equipped with a comprehensive technique of rapid movement. These qualities provide performances exactly suited to the tastes of modern American audiences.

Also, a great expansion of interest in theatre-dance is now developing, and for another decade, with luck, there will be a boom comparable with that we enjoyed about 15 years ago. Recently in New York four companies were dancing simultaneously and each played to a packed house—something that simply has never happened here.

To temper the generalisation a little—all the ballets are not of the first, or even the second, class. When their ideas misfire, American choreographers can achieve some awful mistakes. With professional co-operation from managements and Press officers I was enabled to switch from one theatre to another, catching parts of several programmes containing ballets new to me; so within a few days I looked at two dozen ballets (as well as a fair cross-section of plays) and this mixed bag is clearly representative of the New York theatre today.

The New York City Ballet, housed in the sumptuous new State Theatre, cannot yet "stretch" all the old Balanchine works to, literally, fill this enormous stage. But some ballets gain by concentrating stage-patternings; notably his newest *Variations,* which is a lovely example of his type of musico-balletic crossword puzzle, having many similarities with the earlier *Agon, Monumentum* and *Movements.*

But for narrative-type ballet-making, the old skill revealed in *Prodigal Son, Errante* and *Cotillon,* seems to have dwindled almost to vanishing point. The precise mime and stylised acting required by the theme of his *Harlequinade* is simply not within the company's capacities; nor is *Scotch Symphony* (unknown here) a very happy exercise, though *Serenade* hits the quality of a novel masterpiece in every performance.

American Ballet Theatre, stirring into new life with one of the new Federal Government grants (a novelty in America and approximately similar to our Arts Council's operations), had a fine troupe of dancers, a few soloist-type stars and some familiar ballets on view. Like the comparatively junior Robert Joffrey Ballet, it suffers from organisational problems peculiar to the American scene. In general, few companies command enough finance to run (or to plan) for a year at a time. All costs are astronomical and every season is to some extent an *ad hoc* affair.

For instance, American Ballet Theatre had old works already well known by Robbins and Lander, a classical *pas-de-deux* and, as its only recent novelty, Agnes de Mille's *Wind in the Mountains*. All were finely danced, notably Lander's *Etudes,* gloriously led by Toni Lander and Royes Fernandes. Miss de Mille's work was a sentimental hotch-potch about the charms of 19th century rural life—an afterthought from *Oklahoma!* that should have been left unuttered.

Joffrey's company has been re-formed and expanded many times in recent years; this enforced condition of intermittent life is reflected in repertoire and performance. New ballets are needed to bring in a public (especially for New York) and many choreographers are engaged for each season. Though deplorable as regards long-distance policy, this system has the advantage of keeping balletmaking "on the boil".

For one recent season the company showed three ballets by Joffrey, and eighteen by other choreographers—a diversity of styles and themes that no European group could ever parallel.

Among dance-groups, as distinct from ballet companies, Glen Tetley's showed a trio of his own works, each a blending of balletic and expressionistic styles in a trend which has been growing recently. This marriage of dance methods is desirable because it offers the imaginative choreographer a palette of many subtle colours for use.

Tetley's individual subjects—a lover's duet; a Pierrot life study; a dance-drama of primitive hunting life—were faulted, in my view, by his need to use complex scenic apparatus and furnishings to get his effects. But his choice of music, Schönberg and two modern Americans (Seter and Partos), proved bold and workable.

The Metropolitan Opera Ballet, allowed an occasional all-ballet programme, staged a revival of a Bournonville work and two ballets of

Antony Tudor. Tudor's *Echoing of Trumpets* compares for breadth of theme and precision of characterisation with his earlier *Jardin aux Lilas, Pillar of Fire* and *Undertow*.

His new work *Concerning Oracles* was a three-episode narration of the reactions of people of three distinct periods (16th, early 19th and early 20th centuries) to the impact of magic and demonic influence. Though a superb ballet subject, the production was flawed by inadequate characterisation by most of the cast. The subtlety of dance-acting (as well as of dancing) that this master requires was simply not within the capabilities of this cast.

Gerald Arpino, Anna Sokolow, John Taras, Fernand Nault and Norman Walker were other choreographers showing works new to me, varying from Sokolow's burning contemporaneity in *Opus '65* to Nault's vaudeville-style reworking of *La Fille mal gardée*.

The main distinction these American choreographers share, differentiating them from most European contemporaries, is their acute awareness of modern music and their requiring modern scores specially written for their use. Our large dependence on derivatives from Tchaikovsky, Delibes and misunderstood dodecaphonics, as ballet accompaniments, was one of the more sobering thoughts that I brought back from New York.

# V

## Modern Dance

# Modern Dance

## MODERN DANCE

Preface by A. V. Coton to *Modern Dance: The Jooss-Leeder Method* (1958), by Jane Winearls.

The title "Modern Dance" distinguishes those kinds which have been invented, developed, or adapted from various sources during the past half-century and which are clearly marked by an expressive style quite different from that of other forms such as National, Folk, Musical Comedy or Ballet. No-one can say exactly where or when this began, though Isadora Duncan is usually considered the pioneer of this revolutionary theatre movement.

Unlike most other revolutionaries, Modern Dancers (or the greater proportion of those worth taking seriously) do not waste time denigrating or trying to destroy the system against which they revolted. Ballet has its proper function in the theatre and the apostles and practitioners of Modern Dance think that this newer kind has a place too. As one style of acting, with its ancillary styles of production and stagecraft, will not serve every imaginable dramatic subject, so Modern Dancers consider that ballet cannot deal satisfactorily with all possible dance-subjects.

Isadora Duncan's revolt was against the sterility that had come upon the ballet of her day. She made her own kind of dancing, got talked about and, more important, got her ideas talked about even by such balletic giants as Diaghilev and Fokine. She was so busy being a pioneer, making converts, opening new paths that she did not have the time—nor, think many people, the talent—to create a teaching method for her dance-style, which died either with, or very soon after, her. The whole cultural and artistic atmosphere of Europe and America was at this time ripe for a continuance of her pioneering work and many original thinkers, researchers and idealists laboured, in their various ways, to follow further along the path she had indicated. The record of their work is as fine as that done in any other field of artistic research. The best of them studied and re-studied, as few traditional *maîtres-de-ballet* ever did, every sort of knowledge which might start a new line of thought; the history of dancing, of

135

philosophy, of mathematics, and the sciences of acting, gesture, athletics, acrobatics, were made to yield up notions on the functions of timing, rhythm, space, harmony, which were then experimented with until some point was proved or disproved.

All this has occurred within a space of about sixty years and, in this period, the lives and careers of Rudolf Laban, Mary Wigman, Kurt Jooss, Sigurd Leeder in Europe, and of Ruth St Denis, Ted Shawn, Martha Graham, José Limon, Doris Humphrey in America, are records of ceaseless probing, enquiry, experiment, all equally remarkable for the degree of honesty and selflessness inspiring them. In fact the best training methods of Modern Dance are systems as coherent and logical as the system of ballet training; many of the Moderns accept parts of the technique of ballet, or learn, and then use, its technique in new adaptations fitted for their dancing.

Once we can begin to look at the best work in this field without comparing every aspect of it with ballet, it is clear that Modern Dance has brought a new kind of vitality into the larger art of theatre dancing; it is as logical a growth as the parallel series of experiments that have occurred in such arts as music, painting, sculpture and poetry within the same period.

Part of the legacy of Duncan—for, like all great innovators, her work and reputation have suffered from the excesses committed by the more thoughtless and selfish of her disciples or converts—is a vast regiment of people who can claim (there exists no patenting process to protect the genuine) the name of Modern Dancer, but who are quite unworthy of serious consideration. Usually they are the kind who, in innocent and unsophisticated ways, try to do as Duncan did—to dance freely, spontaneously, out of exuberance and idealism. As she appeared to dispense with any elaborate technical method, so they too imagine that "the urge to self expression" is, in itself, good enough as an apparatus. The record of this kind of Modern Dancer is a burden to be lived down by those who approach their work fully understanding the need to train hard in methods as hard as those belonging to the province of ballet dancing.

Modern Dance, to have any meaning for the spectator or value for the dancer, must be taught as exactly and as continuously as the older method. We assume the existence of natural laws concerning weight, speed, balance, harmony, in the human body and if the dancer is to use that body expressively in a theatre he must be trained to a knowledge of how, when, and how much he will use those laws.

The greater part of Modern Dance development in Europe (in America it started from a different appraisal of the laws of physical movement) grows logically and quite consistently from Rudolf Laban's work as a movement-experimenter. Beginning with studies of ballet, of the work of Delsarte, of many kinds of folk dance, of the laws of mathematics and geometry, he evolved a means of "dissecting out" the basic elements which *create and control* every kind of movement of which the human anatomy is capable. No-one, least of all Laban himself, pretends that everything knowable has been revealed; some of his fellow researchers have, at various points, agreed to disagree with his findings, and have pursued other routes. His work was furthered by the collaboration of Kurt Jooss and Sigurd Leeder, who, starting with the methods and experiments promoted by Laban, carried movement research further until there was evolved the Jooss-Leeder method whereby the dancers of the Ballets Jooss were trained. The importance of this company for over a quarter of a century in the field of Modern Dance is an indication of the value of this method.

There can be no short cut to success in any kind of theatre dancing and the aspiring Modern Dancer needs the same stern discipline, regular work, and devoted commitment to his task as the student of ballet must show. Modern Dance methods, like those of ballet, can be used to train people who have, perhaps, neither ambition nor talent enough to make a professional career. There is too much propaganda which insists that a period of ballet training, whether elementary or intensely advanced technically, is the "best method" of teaching young people how to use their bodies sensibly, dynamically, rewardingly. Modern Dance methods, though unbacked by the glamour (and the disillusion, too) that goes with training in a system of ballet, can give a control, a flexibility, a lyricism, as understandable and usable as those conferred by the same amount of training in ballet.

## THE BALLETS JOOSS IN WARTIME (1944-45)

From *Dance Chronicle*, November, 1944.

The Ballets Jooss is the only one of the internationally touring companies which has appeared on English stages during the war. The last splitting-off of forces amongst the "Russian Ballet" companies had resulted, in 1938, in the reconstitution of the Monte Carlo Ballet with Massine as artistic director and principal choreographer. This company was to have given a Covent Garden season in September, 1939, when several new Massine works would have been seen, but for the inevitable last-day cancellation.

The Ballets Jooss was the one international unit which had its headquarters in this country, and its autumn provincial tour of 1939 was carried out despite the difficulties which followed the events of 3 September. It was decided to carry out commitments already made, and in December the company, minus Kurt Jooss and Sigurd Leeder, sailed for America. For almost three years they played everything from Metropolitan seasons to one-night stands in Canada, the United States, Central and South America, covering about 30,000 miles en route. The separation which Kurt Jooss had to endure might have been a serious artistic set-back for any other sort of ballet company dependent for works on one principal choreographer. But the Ballets Jooss repertory with the addition of one new work (*Drums Sound in Hackensack*, Agnes de Mille) proved on this extensive tour that the truly dramatic ballet is strong enough to appeal, and continuously appeal, to audiences, without there being felt the ceaseless necessity of adding novelties and revivals—a process which occupies so much of the time, money and talents of the orthodox ballet groups.

The South American tour revealed an extraordinary interest in these works which had not hitherto been seen south of Panama. Such important cities as Rio de Janeiro, Montevideo and Buenos Aires offered bookings for two or three weeks which were expanded into a month, six weeks and eight weeks when the seasons opened; return dates were played in some of these places midway through the tour. In all, thirteen South American cities were played and the pioneering tour was not without difficulties. One leading dancer went out of action in the first weeks through a leg injury, made a long ocean voyage back to the United States for treatment, and was recovered just as the tour came to a close and was waiting to welcome the returning dancers into New York from Venezuela. In some parts, railways were impracticable if timetables were to be adhered to, and the company with all its equipment travelled hundred of miles by lorry, spending days and nights on the road, on the journey through the wet-green forests and mountain ranges of upper Amazonia. The conditions were comparable in strenuousness with those in which some ENSA units have worked on various far-flung battle-fronts.

Some dancers have, since the beginning of this tour, settled in North and South America, and in some places have established dance schools where the strongest European form of Modern Dance can be canalised into the flow of the contemporary American dance-world.

After the return from South America, further playing in New York and some touring occupied the period until plans for the re-shipping of everyone surviving back to England could be completed. This was, of course, after America had entered the war, when shipping space was scarce, waiting lists were long, and many voyages ended tragically in mid-Atlantic. After some months the company assembled in Cambridge, which became the new headquarters for the company; the happy association with Dartington Hall which had lasted since 1934 now ended with the dissolution of that establishment by its founder, Mr L. K. Elmhirst.

Some works in the repertoire have not been given since 1939 and 1940, for the same reason that similar restriction has been imposed on most ballet companies, limitation of personnel. The composition of the company, a relatively small group considering the scope of the works, the length of the company's existence and the arduous nature of its touring life, has varied less in five war years than that of any other group of comparative importance.

Now after two years' wartime work in England, the company is as artistically sound and as technically integrated as ever before. This is, in a sense, an inevitability, as only those possessed of a great capacity for hard work and a singularly depersonalised attitude towards dancing can stay the course under the aegis of Kurt Jooss. The Ballets Jooss has never been a comfortable background for glamour girls or for dance careerists: it has meant an atmosphere of tough training work and rehearsals on a scale that, amongst traditional ballet companies, a Massine would demand —but with much less sound and fury going on in the background or around the stage door.

The Ballets Jooss is at an important stage in its artistic growth for now its revolution, following the classic order of revolutions, is established: the noisiest opposition is quietened: the change of ideology is becoming acceptable; and the developmental phase now opens out. That phase is marked by the emergence of choreographers, trained by Jooss, who in turn will train, direct and influence other choreographers. Within the next few months, new ballets will appear from three choreographers in the company, and their artistic value will be in ratio to the means whereby the creators successive to Jooss can expand, modify, and individually colour the dance-drama formula which he has established, without their conceding anything to the traditional form. Jooss has shown how much can be safely taken from the orthodox canon for dance-drama usage: the traditional method is now due to absorb from the Jooss system some of the close-moulded mime and dance technique which he developed and demonstrated so superbly in *The Big City* and *Prodigal Son,* and, most movingly of all, in *Pandora,* his most refined creation.

From *Dance Chronicle,* April, 1944 and August, 1945.

The major distinction between the work of what may be called "the orthodox choreographer" and Kurt Jooss is not to be found in the widely differing technical media, but in the method of approach to the function of choreography. Apart from a few works in the genre of *ballet psychologique*, all the achievements since Petipa that we know have as their primary choreographic aim the satisfying of an audience's need for visual and aural beauties. Whatever your or my definition of beauty may be, this aim is the prime consideration: the successful choreographer satisfies, with the one synthesis, many different people's different aesthetic needs.

Jooss is little concerned with what might be called "the final appeal to the senses" of a series of moments of beauty wrought out of music, dance, applied stagecraft and dancer's personality. He is a realist theatre-artist in the same sense as Aldous Huxley defines Homer as a realist writer in his essay "The Whole Truth": a writer unable and unwilling to disguise from his reader the fact that Tragedy and Comedy are never found in undiluted form in real life—or in great art. Farce and Agony invade one another's spheres of influence in every conceivable emotional situation. The clown twists his ankle, or a brickbat falls on his head, just as he reaches the climax of his funniest story: the guests knock at Macbeth's gate a moment after a revolting murder has been committed, and are greeted by a drunken manservant who regales them with trenchant observations on the art and craft of fornication.

In his work Kurt Jooss shows that he is unable to accept that a form of theatre should be escapist: bearing in mind that some forms of realism, unacceptable to the many, provide escapism for the few. *The Big City, The Green Table, Spring Tale, Prodigal Son*—and now, *Pandora*—owe their theatrical success to their dual effectiveness in giving emotional satisfaction in performance, and in dropping a leaven into the subconscious which again and again prompts our (possibly uneasy) reflections on the outcome of the permanent struggle between Good and Evil.

Let it not be thought that this implies a superiority of one sort of choreographic approach: it emphasises a difference. We all have need of a soothing syrup now and then as we cut our worldly wisdom teeth on the hard facts of life; the great thing is to know when our teeth are strong enough to gnaw at the bones of experience. Even those who prefer a Theatre of Escapism cannot always succeed in leaving their brains at the door of the auditorium, and if one reacts to the emotional stimulus spontaneously one cannot fail to be touched, at some level, by the ideas latent and expressed which form the basis and framework of Jooss' great ballets.

In watching *The Big City* or *The Green Table*, the keener one's emotional response the faster comes the reaction prompting the question: Where have I met such a situation? How much is my life touched by events like these? The spectator's appreciation of the stage happenings is heightened because (whether he knows it then or not) he is in unison with the characters. The effect is not one of transposition (X in the audience becoming at the high emotional moments Hamlet or Romeo or Cordelia), but of correlation (X realising his or her blood-brotherhood with all the other Hamlets, Romeos, Cordelias, Portias and Giselles). The residue of this sort of theatrical experience is not the memory of a shared identity, when one *was* for a moment Hamlet or Cordelia, but the reflection that one is always something of Hamlet and Cordelia: and this something is affecting the pattern of every moment of one's living. Because this touching at a deeper level happens integrally with a satisfying aesthetic experience, it forms a positive, if unconscious, antidote to that *hubris* with which we are all a little affected.

Except the divertissement-ballet or the dance-suite nearly every ballet that tells a story tells a story of good triumphing over evil. Not always with the simplicity or the vividness of the best Romantic Period works and the Fokine fairy-play moralities: but generally in clear-cut terms, with the aesthetic interest growing out of characterisations of the rival forces made potent by the choreographic layout of *pas seuls, adagios* and gesture-behaviour.

*Pandora,* using a free reading of the myth, emphasises that the struggle between Good and Evil is a perpetual one. It goes on everywhere all the time; it happens because Good and Evil are complementary parts of the same moral sense. The emphasis figures in this ballet are Pandora, "a beautiful woman without a soul, sent by the jealous gods with the gift of a box to mankind", and Psyche "the personification of the soul and of unselfish devotion".

In a pattern of six movements, the ebb and flow of greed, pride, despair, exultation, humility, sorrow and desolation motivate the dancers, who personify The Youth, The Strong Man, The Monsters, The Young Men and Women, The Elders, etc. A story of great dramatic intensity is unfolded, wherein The Go-Getter lusts and struggles, The Strong Man is bewildered, silent, angry and vengeful, Pandora lures, beguiles, amazes and conquers; while Psyche inspires, leads, ennobles, is cast down. The Youth is earthy, simple, raw, The Elders cautious, humble and defenceless. Hideous Monsters, stuff of dreams and raw reality, strike terror and misery into the people.

The whole process is exciting, moving and aesthetically and psychologically so balanced that, while we have the sense of a certain experience which we have lived through while watching the performance, we have the calm quiet following a nervous satiation; which preludes much cogitation. We know that The Youth, Pandora and The Elders, the Machines and the Go-Getters were realities because in the performance we caught echoes of all the people we have ever known who had any of the qualities informing Pandora and her victims. And we cannot fail to identify in ourselves some of the simplicity and humility of the Youth, the sadism of The Go-Getter, the power-lust and destructiveness of Pandora.

The ballet is a transmutation into fresh theatrical terms of the stuff of a dozen tragedies, hammered into our attention by the complex, compelling and strange patterns of movement whilst our receptivity is kept keyed up by the deliberately unmelodic, variably rhythmic score for two pianos and percussion.


## JOOSS AT ESSEN (1951)

From *Ballet*, September, 1951.

Werden is a suburb of Essen and as far removed in appearance and atmosphere from that industrial centre as Chipping Campden or Thaxted is from, say, Leeds or Glasgow. Six miles from the city's centre, it is surrounded by lush forests and hills, contains many pleasant old buildings and an impressive school. The school is housed in the 'abbey', a massive baroque structure which has been in turn an abbey, a barracks, a warehouse and—under Hitler—a prison. Today it is administered by the municipality of Essen and its halls, classrooms, offices and theatre afford working space for schools of music, drama and dance, and an academy of crafts and plastic arts. Several English and European provincial cities support arts-and-crafts schools but few of them have the specialist staff, amplitude of space and facilities, and variety of subjects that Essen offers for the instruction and entertainment of its citizens. It was in Essen that Kurt Jooss worked in the late 1920s and from that city went the first 'Ballets Jooss' to present *The Green Table* at the International Choreographic Congress in Paris in 1932. The school at Werden is full of activity and the Dance School under Jooss' direction is there to provide the foundation for the newest version of The Ballets Jooss: after its first two years' course the school was able to present a number of trained dancers (the majority of whom had already undergone training and acquired dance experience in other cities and schools) to the company. Early in June the re-born Ballets Jooss gave its initial performances in the Essen City Theatre, presenting two revivals and two new works.

On Friday, 8 June, a company of twenty-four dancers appeared in a programme consisting of *Big City, 1926*; *Fantasie*; *Colombinade* and *The*

*Green Table.* The leading dancers are Noelle de Mosa, Ulla Soederbaum, Hans Züllig and Rolf Alexander, the twenty others are drawn mainly from Germany, Switzerland, Holland and Chile, with single representatives of France, England, Poland and Java. The two early ballets fully justify their retention in the repertoire; they remain perfect dance-drama expressions of their subjects—a period piece which perfectly mirrors a cross-section of life in a modern industrial city, and a work which is probably this century's most persuasive piece of polemical theatrecraft. *The Green Table* seems—unfortunately—likely to remain both topical and controversial for the next half century.

Jooss' new ballet, *Colombinade,* has a brief programme note suggesting that the audience views these fantasy characters, creating their own more complicated fantasies, with sympathy but also with wide-open eyes; an instruction which makes no explanation of the ballet but encourages the spectator to draw what conclusions he will from this odd series of nightmarish adventures. Harlequin, Columbine, Clown and Pierrot are joined in their gambols by several type figures—An Unknown Lady, a Big Business Man, a Debutante, a Spiv and a kind of comic Tyl Eulenspiegel disguised as The Footballer. The lyric and satiric incidents which flow out of the conjunction of these several characters are given an additional 'dimension' by the appearance later in the ballet of a series of doubles or *Doppelgänger* of The Unknown Lady, The Manageress, The Spiv and The Big Business Man. The climax event is the bringing together by Pierrot of The Debutante and the *ersatz* Eulenspiegel. The work is a mixture of romance, farce and satire; the music, sometimes deadly appropriate, occasionally unrelated, is drawn from popular and unknown Strauss pieces; the décor and costumes are the work of Rochus Gliese.

*Fantasie* is Hans Züllig's second ballet, described as a composition for two soloists and group and arranged on the F-minor Fantasy of Schubert; its abstract décor and romantic-abstract costumes are also by Gliese, and here he has admirably sustained the choreographer's intention, where, in *Colombinade,* he overworked the fantastic to the extent of providing some of the most shockingly ugly dresses ever danced in. The work can be described as an elaborately developed *pas de deux* in non-classical dance idiom, with a constantly changing framework which is provided by the double *corps de ballet*—eight females and six male dancers. The quality of the movement throughout is simple, amazingly fluid and lyrical; there are almost no remarkably difficult steps or movements, trick dance episodes or virtuoso passages. The choreography throughout looks unbelievably simple, unforced, inevitable to this music; it results in one of the most satisfying abstract ballets seen in many years. Its greatest point, I think, is that it shows convincingly that a type of dance idiom totally unlike the classical ballet in vocabulary and syntax can be made to yield up a dance spectacle as satisfying—within its own aesthetic terms—as any of the 'pure dancing' ballets of Balanchine or Ashton. *Fantasie* is a triumph for the company which created it, in that it shows these dancers capable of making pure lyrical dancing as effective, in this particular idiom, as their dramatic dancing is effective.

The two chief roles were danced by Ulla Soederbaum and Hans Züllig, who were supporters of two principal roles in the other new ballet also. The average dancing experience in Ballets Jooss works of the four dancers from earlier days is about fifteen years each; the intensity of dramatic and lyrical quality with which they infuse their roles sets them on a level beyond that of the rest of the group, and yet the comparative differences between top- and second-rank dancers here is less obvious in performances than it would be in any other kind of dance company, because the works depend for effect, throughout, much more on projection of character and personality than on projection of technical mastery of the dance-role. In these initial performances (8, 10 and 11 June) some dancers were giving first performances after several years' inactivity, some were dancing for the first time on this continent, and a few were appearing in public for the first time. Rolf Alexander danced Death in *The Green Table,* Noelle de Mosa created the role of The Debutante, Ulla Soederbaum that of Colombine, and Züllig was Harlequin in *Columbinade,* while Soederbaum and Züllig shared the central roles in *Fantasie.*

When the school was reorganized, Jooss called in a first-rate Cecchetti method teacher, Laura Maris, who had worked with the earlier company at Cambridge some years ago: Züllig is an accomplished teacher and has undergone considerable periods of classical ballet training at various times. The work of these two amongst the six teaching staff is not directed to turning Jooss dancers into imitation classical dancers; rather, the most flexible manner of applying the brilliance of Italian-style ballet pedagogy is mingled with the basic eurhythmic and eukinetic dance tuition. Both give classes of inspired quality, full of invention of *enchaînements*; on occasion the exercises devised to merge balletic precision and Modern Dance suppleness evolve into mass choreographic patterns not unlike the big geometrical figures sometimes noted in Balanchine's abstract ballets. Far from, as one horrified balletomane suggested, 'putting the Jooss dancers on *pointes*', this mixing of the best in classical and modern training methods helps to bring one small degree nearer a fusion of the two idioms which, it seems to me, has very nearly been established in Züllig's new ballet.

The company will appear intermittently at this year's Ruhr Festival in Recklinghausen and will not dance regularly until a second programme is prepared; this is to consist of a revival of Züllig's *Le Bosquet* and two new Jooss works, *Dithyrambus* and *Night Train,* and with other revivals added will give enough repertoire for the long tour of Germany, Holland and Switzerland which begins this autumn: by next May the company should appear in Paris.

At this point of its re-emergence from many difficulties, it is proper to ask what is the artistic strength and the future development of the Ballets Jooss. We have to realise that this particular section of the twentieth century revolution in theatre dance comprises a fresh kind of dance idiom, a school of dance style (with several foreign branches) and a repertory of works—the whole an achievement worked out between 1919 and 1932. During twenty years the company has been dominated, quite inevitably, by one choreographer, the first. Züllig occupies the interesting historical position of being the first capable disciple following in the steps of the prime innovator. The test of any new departure in idiomatic or technical practice in any kind of art is its power to develop and proliferate when it passes into the control of the first wave of artists following the original creator or innovator. By his second ballet, *Fantasie* (created six years after his first), Züllig shows, I think conclusively, that he is a master choreographer in this field of dance. We now await two important—and I believe historically necessary—developments: Züllig's ability to create both more abstract works and his own brand of dance-drama; and the first successful works of at least one good choreographer who must come out of the present group of dancers. At the earliest neither of these possibilities can show before the spring or summer of 1952—and by that time the Ballets Jooss may be on the way to their first season in England since their post-war re-formation in Essen.

## MARTHA GRAHAM (1967)

From *The Daily Telegraph*, 26 April, 1967.
Martha Graham's recent London season with her dance company showed the ballets and the dancers as rich in variety and also as variable in quality as on her previous visits. Much the strongest impression of the season was its air of finality—its suggestion of the total flowering of everything that the name of Graham has meant.

It is clear that on the day she ceases to create new works the company will at once begin to disintegrate—which is a pity; but dance history shows that no *avant-garde* company has ever survived the creative span of its leader. Such innovators never tolerate choreographic competition and so the greater part of their artistic worth dies with them. Most modern American free-form choreographers have come out of Graham's studio and/or company and each of them (Hawkins, Sokolow, Dudley, Cunningham and Lang) has promoted a choreographic style reaching farther and farther away from hers.

In the Graham system a small range of themes is dealt with through a special (and limited) vocabulary of movements: music has little function except to provide an "atmosphere surround" for the dancing. Visually, the works dispense with painted scenery but employ a three-dimensional type of staging in which symbolic objects in fantasy shapes do service as screens, pedestals, thrones, battlements and so on.

Costumes, often of extreme beauty of cut and colour, are usually of Miss Graham's own devising and by now form a convention of their own, with the males all but nude and the females usually encased in something like a ballroom dress of the 'thirties.

In these spectacles the impact comes much more from the three-dimensional, sculptural quality of the movement rather than from clear-cut characterisation, mimic action or sheer dance exhibitionism. The tendency towards heavy dramas of blood, vengeance and lust, usually from Greek mythology or the Bible, outweighs the lyrical side of Miss Graham's genius. Few of her works are openly comic or satiric, though there are sardonic overtones in some of the lyrical ones. The most disturbing aspect of the entire canon is that, while her works are largely supposed to be motivated by "ideas about love", they show a ceaseless concern with lust and a sympathetic feeling for mere animalistic sexuality.

A fair balance sheet on the company, at this last viewing, would show as follows:

> *FOR*—A completely new method of creating dance movement; a new mode of using stage-space, lighting, properties and costumes; and a new method of choreography, in which the dancing is perpetually intermingled with both stylised and naturalistic gesture and movement.

> *AGAINST*—The usually characterless music which rarely allies itself specifically with its accompanying movement; the limited number of steps (meaning actual movements whereby the dancer propels himself from place to place, or passes through the air); and the even more limited kind of gesture used; and, of course, the above-mentioned small range of ideas out of which Miss Graham has created one hundred and forty different works during about forty years.

A careful look at the achievement of the past twenty years suggests two very important factors in her work which have significantly changed the notion of theatre-dance in our time. Like Duncan before her, Graham's whole choreographic activity has been a campaign to make dancing significantly theatrical as a form of communication—rather than merely entertaining. Her big asset has been the movement style which she invented and which is being taught more and more widely. But this style has also provided her greatest limitation.

Paradoxically, at this moment of her widest acclaim here, her system and her repertoire have displayed their weaknesses as well as their strengths very clearly. Nearly all the ballets would be utterly banal unless danced with the power and vivacity that this company commands, and if seen without the benefit of these décors and costumes.

The company's London success with the younger generation has, I think, rested on the fact that, whereas traditional ballets as danced performances have a timeless quality in visualisation, Graham's works are "pure period". Their themes, music and costumes are the embodiment of the far-away glamour, the adventurousness, the quaintness, of the two pre-war decades.

And precisely at this period her teaching and training method is being assiduously taught here. However, we are still a long way off the time when the Graham teaching or choreographic modes can be digested into our native theatre-dance system.

The paradox is further pointed when we note that no choreographer *anywhere* creates Graham-type ballets. A future for the whole concept of "Graham Style" depends on the just-possible revitalisation of her creative ability into a fresh field of theme—a believable contingency now that her own dancing days are almost ended.

From *The Daily Telegraph*, 5 April, 1967.

The season opened at the Saville Theatre with three familiar works displaying the varied qualities of this splendid team as preliminaries to Miss Graham's appearance in her newest drama.

To an extent rare in other dance systems, the value of any step or gesture depends not so much on the shape or quality of the movement as on the absolute degree of dynamism or lyricism supplied by the dancer.

This means a mode much dependent on the performer's unfailing disciplines, control, and commitment to the role.

These spectacles are no showcases for brilliant performers, but make their effects by forcing the dancers to exploit character and situation in starkly luminous but rigidly-controlled movement.

*Cortège of Eagles* is a version of the tale of the Fall of Troy, with the Hecuba of Miss Graham an epitome of all the lustful and pitiless heroines of classical literature.

Loaded with daringly novel décor, costumes and properties by Isamu Noguchi, the story, urgent and dramatic though many of its episodes are, lacks an effective visual climax. So many betrayals, agonising combats and mourning processions do not coalesce into a moment of high, ecstatic resolution of the tragic tale.

Miss Graham's unique vocabulary of movement could, if performed by people less suited and less expert, often seem limited, with its angular and jerking movements and the heavily staccato style of execution. But the team has high talents trained to a hairsbreadth and wholly disciplined for these dance subjects as wrought in Miss Graham's imagination.


## MERCE CUNNINGHAM (1964 and 1966)

1964
From *The Daily Telegraph*, 28 July, 1964, 30 July, 1964,
1 August, 1964 and 6 August, 1964.

Every true theatrical pioneer opens a legitimate path towards the future of his art and, inevitably, overreaches himself. Biting off more than he can chew is his daily occupation, and the frequent resulting artistic indigestion is what the public witnesses.

Merce Cunningham, a genuine pioneer, with his Dance Company, opened last night at Sadler's Wells a season whose label must inescapably be "controversial".

He deliberately abandons the normal conventions of ballet-making by using movement, music, costumes and décor in partly organised dissociation—not in organised association. The elements are not made to blend and are meant to make their impacts separately on us. The dancing is mostly a series of cautious moves into positions which are then exploited in fascinating slow-motion actions. The music is mostly a non-rhythmic and non-melodic continuum of orchestral "sounds". It is played in a choreographic vacuum. It does not need to, and scarcely ever does, fit the steps and gestures.

The style contains some splendid acrobatics and poses based on the best of ballet and modern dancing. Here and there in the four ballets there are beautiful groupings and brilliant short episodes.

Mr Cunningham preaches and practises the notion that dancing does not need the aid of music or story, or even characterisation. It is meant to be sufficient in itself but, artistically, he cheats us. He cannot pretend that a ballet is a "story" about people in emotional conflict when the choreography and the music are changed arbitrarily at each performance, so inevitably reducing the dancers to mere mechanical technicians.

The company's several gimmicks include non-use of music, use of non-music, and a great reliance on the possible theatrical impact of the inconsequential.

But dancing (least of all the arts, surely) cannot be divorced from some form of continuous organisation and pattern (however esoteric). These dance conditions are, in fact, present in these programmes but too deliberately overlaid with choreographic theories that wear rather thin after the first half-dozen ballets.

*Nocturnes,* the twelfth new work shown by the company, is almost wholly successful as a comprehensible ballet. It shows men and women involved in relationships which even suggest deep emotional interest in one another. This is so far against the choreographer's dance philosophy (which is, that our interest should focus wholly on the movement for its own sake) that he will give me no thanks for this verdict.

It has recognisable music of Erik Satie and its white and silver décor by Robert Rauschenberg might have looked quaintly novel in 1934. It shows three couples in patterned episodes of contact: touching, meeting, parting, reacting, with occasional moments of beautiful figurings.

*Cross Currents* was given its première* and fits the general Cunningham pattern in showing a trio of male and two females in disconnected episodes of movement which, by hit or miss methods, may say something to us about what the performers appear to be involved in.

The company's work is, historically, a necessary purgative for the whole of theatre dance art and the audience subscribes unconsciously to the atmosphere like so many spectators of a laboratory experiment.

Cunningham displays a courageous determination to make us accept this new kind of anti-ballet. He is not content with simply (in the words of his manifesto) "presenting activity". Like any conventional ballet-maker he explains too much about the nature of the dance spectacle, the quality of the accompanying sounds and the function of the décor. It all sounds cautiously apologetic in case we should be too mystified by the weird movements.

If his works were as iconoclastic as his supporters pretend, surely he would present them for what they are, the inconsequential patterns made by moving bodies in time and space. He should be willing to let this sort

*31 July, 1964

of choreography, which really is existentialism in dance, speak entirely for itself. The actions, gestures, unbalanced steps, hops, jumps and beautiful moments of cunning balance are accompanied, in no fixed time relation, by a series of musical jokes which are just not quaint enough to be really enjoyable sick jokes.

The whole spectacle is a rare experience though it does not aim at or achieve the sort of emotional or aesthetic effect that a normal ballet performance can create.

As one mystified lady said to her companion in the interval: "It isn't very much like *Giselle*, is it?"

1966
From *The Daily Telegraph*, 24 November, 1966 and 30 November, 1966.
Nothing in the practice of the arts ages so fast as novelty, and all too often the avant-garde of last year is tonight's old hat. Merce Cunningham with his company of dancers (here two years ago) opened the season last night at the Saville Theatre with three of his highly personal compositions.

Mr Cunningham's unchanged formula is to bring together arbitrarily several kinds of movement (some of it actual dancing), tapes of electronic and mechanical noises, and a variety of staging, designs and costumes— none of them inspired by, deriving from, or logically related to the others. The resulting "action" is to be taken as having no specific or generalised meaning. The spectacle is on its highest as on its lowest levels simply Mr Cunningham's assault on, or wooing of, your nervous system and sensibility.

The programme included two new works, *Place* and *Variations V*, together with the previously seen *Nocturnes*.

Neither of the new pieces showed much coherence of structure. *Place's* most noticeable visual gimmick was an elaborate handing around of the female dancers by the males like so many parcels of meat—done up in cellophane, too.

The second work involved some mixed high-school gymnastics, imitation judo and bicycle riding, with a sound track notable for its plurality of decibels. This is accompanied by a décor of deliberately badly-projected films.

But with almost no variations in techniques (only in their densities) Mr Cunningham showed us all this in 1964; notably *Nocturnes*, which now is as obvious as any cautious European ballet of the period 1950-60.

His "ballets" legitimately belong to the epoch of the dramas of Beckett and the music of Stockhausen although his architectural method is to despise foundations, attach a few floors and ceilings to three walls and hope to sell the product as a building.

Yet the accidents of his non-associative method of hanging together notions, movements, lighting and various types of noise can now and then produce an effect.

*Winterbranch* shows the performers groping, wrestling, sliding mostly in sepulchral darkness, then suddenly bursting into chain-or-circle figures which hint at dancing.

The part silence, part uproar, which is the accompaniment, contributes to the work's eerie power—a kind of hell of boringness, as in Sartre's *Huis Clos*.

*Suite for Five* and *How to Pass, Kick, Fall and Run* are Cunningham pure (almost) and plain (comparatively)—being series of alternate slow-motion and fast-action runs, gyrations, jumps and some occasional fancy tumbling.

The first has a noise accompaniment, the second a spoken commentary of American folksy or humorous situations.

So near, yet so far from immediate theatricality, these confections have the mechanical relentlessness and the inhuman regularity of the computer's products.


## PAUL TAYLOR (1966 and 1968)

### 1966

*The Daily Telegraph, 7 July, 1966.*

As its main contribution to the Holland Festival, the Paul Taylor Dance Company of New York presented *Orbs,* a long ballet in free-style dance form, at Utrecht yesterday.

Using most, but not all, of three late Beethoven quartets for its 95 minutes of dancing, this "planetary ballet" depicts the interactions of Sun, Moon, Earth, Venus, Mars and Pluto.

Such splendid notions can make viable theatrical effect only through choreography of unique invention which can justify such oddities of music, of staging and of a small cast as were here used.

The major factor working against choreographic completeness was the unnecessary length. On the dance stage there are significant differences between choreographic time, clock time and spectators' time.

This music, as episode followed episode in Mr Taylor's familiar choreographic formulas, seemed more and more irrelevant. The Earth episode (informal contemporary clothes) dwindled into a small thin joke as the dancers cavorted through scenes of betrothal, a wedding, and a drunken feast.

The more abstract scenes hinted at fragments of the various planetary legends though their dramatic content was ill-defined and ill-realised.

Largeness of imagination in ballet must be immutably blended with an equal largeness of clarified inventiveness. Lurking inside this well-padded concept was a skeletonic notion of a ballet on cosmic powers.

Some ruthless pruning and rearranging would probably result in a dramatically forceful spectacle. As it stands, *Orbs* is an artistic mishap; too literally shapeless and therefore looking pretentious.

Three shorter ballets, *Junction, Three Epitaphs* and *Duet,* were brilliantly danced and each hit its dramatic or aesthetic target dead on centre, precisely because they said in dance exactly what was worth saying in exactly the right amount of time.

## 1968
*The Daily Telegraph*, 13 June, 1968.

The splendours of the best kind of non-traditional theatre dancing and some of the system's most obstinate errors were equally revealed in the Paul Taylor Dance Company programme last night. Appearing in the Theatre Royal at St. Helens for their only English engagement, this New York company presented two premières and two works familiar from earlier English visits.

The latter were *Aureole* and *Three Epitaphs*, the novelties were *Post Meridian* to electronic music by Evelyn De Boeck, and *Lento* to Haydn's Opus 51.

In this free-style mode of non-ballet dance Mr Taylor has made a clear personal idiom in which he can create lyrical figures, long phrases and static groupings of a most sumptuous beauty, and the staccato movements usually have great dynamic force.

No décor is used, and body tights, usually with painted patternings, are the regular garb of these barefoot dancers, who are fine instruments for this dance mode.

*Post Meridian* and *Lento* are not in any programmatic sense about anything; overtly non-dramatic, they can be interpreted as anyone pleases —so the commonest reaction is of straight aesthetic pleasure or a stimulation of the senses by the changing interplay of light, colour, movement and music.

Mr Taylor uses a quite small vocabulary of movements; certain kinds of jumping and sliding steps and held poses occur over and over again in all the ballets. In between, the dancers move quite naturalistically from one position to another—and the visual excitement or the dramatic aura is instantly deflated.

Essentially this means that this is an undeveloped choreographic style; its thinness and its repetitions work against the often very effective originality of Mr Taylor's movement structure and the music.

## ALVIN AILEY IN EDINBURGH (1968)

From *The Dancing Times*, October, 1968.

It is one of the hard facts of ballet—and of ballet criticism—that the virtues of good choreography will shine through the thinness of very bad dancing, whereas no amount of fine dancing can cover up the poverty of unoriginal choreography. This consideration was clearly emphasised in the Edinburgh performances of Ailey's company, as it had been equally apparent a few weeks earlier during the visit to St. Helens of the Paul Taylor Dance Company.

Both these seasons pinpointed the entire problem of what can be identified as the conflicts and correspondences between traditional ballet and Contemporary Free Dance. No major figure of the "Modern" movement has shown an equal strength with any major creator in the traditional field. However big the output, they do not command a range of dance-images, a diversity of scenarios, nor a width of expressive styles comparable with the methods of, say, Fokine, Massine, Balanchine, Tudor, Ashton and Cranko, or even half-a-dozen lesser creators in the conventional mode of ballet.

It might be too easy an explanation to say that the too-frequent similarities—visual, aural and narrative—among their works are due to the limited range of dance movements that each uses. Although this factor has to be considered, is not the real explanation that every one of these pioneers (and some have been genuine explorers into rare fields of movement-usage) has come to a point at which the ideas, the technique, even the motivation for their creation of ballets, have reached their fullest expansion? The problem for all of them is that their choreographic notions are based on a *special* movement technique which each one has invented or adapted or developed, which is for ever a personal signature and from which they cannot—dare not try to?—escape. You cannot confuse a ballet of Martha Graham with one by Merce Cunningham, Anna Sokolow, Talley Beatty, Paul Taylor, Glen Tetley, or Alvin Ailey; each one's style

bears certain idiosyncrasies which cannot, under risk of an accusation of plagiarism, be used by any of the others.

During the Ailey company's earlier London visits we saw an exciting amalgam of novel themes, unusual music, compact choreography, all supported by exceptionally fine Negro dancing (and "Negro dancing" means something quite unique and not to be looked at as derogatory to either white or coloured dancers). The three Edinburgh programmes of twelve ballets included eight works new here, including two world premières (*Quintet* and *Knoxville: Summer 1915*). Not one item was a truly fresh choreographic utterance; each was an unconscious copy of, or parallel with, ideas used by other contemporary dance choreographers —sometimes the creator was plagiarising himself. Good lighting was used but mostly the music was disappointing. Alvin Ailey and many of his fellows, including Talley Beatty and John Fealy, seem to accept that any piece of modern Jazz (particularly "Blues") is automatically a piece of stage dance music. Perhaps the use of such music, which rarely has any recognisable organic shape, seems right to the choreographer of contemporary Negro subjects because it always seems atmospherically suitable. Unhappily, the atmosphere projected by the various scores is the same one—that curious mingling of defiance and defeatism that colours so many of these ballets. At the risk of an accusation of some sort of race prejudice, let me state that no minority, racial or religious, whether Negro, Jewish, Mahomedan, Armenian, Vietnamese or any other, is expressing itself artistically justly if there is constant emphasis on the degradation (real or imagined) that it has undergone, without equal reference to its unique achievements and victories.

Together with this unselective choice of music went too much imprecision and casualness of choreography. I do not suggest that non-Negro choreographers automatically have a superiority of craftsmanship in this field (we have all seen far too many incoherent ballets made by familiar European and American dance-arrangers). What did most strongly emerge from this repertoire was the consideration that a dance-theatre wholly preoccupied with the problems, joys, triumphs and defeats of the Negro in a context of American contemporary living does not encourage boldness of idea, width of vision or deep examination into how much can be done with stage dancing.

The most pleasing work was still Ailey's *Revelations* and it was not wholly accidental that the sweetness, lyricism and vivacity owed so much to the superbly apt music; this was an arrangement of a dozen or so familiar spirituals whose dynamic and subtlety were marvellously matched with highly sympathetic choreography. Plenty of other works of similar composition have shown an unbearable sentimentality, but here Ailey's sure handling of the delicate emotional power of the music led to an equally delicate choreographic emotion. Lucas Hoving, the only non-Negro choreographer represented, made of *Icarus* an exciting version of the myth, seen as a three-sided conflict between Icarus, Daedalus and The Sun. Miguel Godreau, Kelvin Rotardier and Judith Jamison extracted every morsel of symbolic power and emotional rapport from the situation.

*Knoxville: Summer 1915,* centred on Godreau, who, though of mixed French, Spanish and Carib Indian blood, looks more powerfully Negro than anyone else around. This atmospheric piece proved to be a minor-keyed and quite unconscious essay in the mode of Antony Tudor, yet its soft and gentle theme was neatly illuminated by Ailey's suave choreography. Geoffrey Holder's *Prodigal Prince* never got off the ground, as a narrative about Hector Hippolite, an actual Haitian 20th-century painter. The accounts of his efforts to be recognised as a painter and his activities as a high priest of Voodoo could not be blended into effective dance-acting, though there were some impressive episodes of voodoo magic and possession.

Talley Beatty, the choreographer of *Black District,* has an admirable streak of choreographic energy, much more intuitive than disciplined, as many of his works show. But this "protest" ballet was loaded with too many self-conscious episodes about the niceness and the horror of contemporary American Negro life, stressing anti-Negro violence to the point of hysteria.

As well as Godreau's superb quality in every appearance, there was the same excellent professionalism as London audiences have seen from both Dudley Williams and Kelvin Rotardier. Together with the high artistry of the beautifully sultry Consuelo Atlas and the fine dramatic dancing of Judith Jamison, this trio provided the purest pleasures in a repertoire which constantly emphasised that the whole value of a contemporary Negro dance theatre needs to be re-examined—thoroughly and honourably and quickly.

# VI

## What's the Use of Critics?

# What's the Use of Critics?

On 22 February, 1950 Coton read a paper entitled
'What's the Use of Critics?' to the Music Section of
The Critics' Circle, London, and this was later published
by *The Music Review* (August 1950). The paper is given here
in a somewhat shortened form. Coton was at that time what he
terms "a comparatively junior member of the Circle"—he had
been elected in 1948. He retained a consistent and practical
interest in this body and was one of the very few ballet
critics who served a term as its President (1961).

We here all know that the difficulties and frustrations, and the very slender
rewards we gain by our work, are things which would simply not be
tolerable unless we were continuously sustained by our certain knowledge
that the function of criticism is an absolutely necessary one to the organisation of the arts, particularly in the world as we find it today. How
much the public interested in the arts knows of our feeling about our work
is a thing none of us knows for certain; but there is enough reaction of one
sort and another to convince even the most hardened sceptic amongst us,
that—whatever black words are said, whatever black looks given when
we are recognised in public places—we have a place in the world of art as
surely as the artist, the manager and the impresario.

We could, I suppose, spend a great deal of time in possibly usefully
disputing our several definitions of those two key words—"art" and
"critic". I take it that each of us has had what we may call "a good
working definition" of both the word "critic" and the word "art" in the
forefront of his mind ever since the very first day he *didn't* receive a
rejection-slip. These "working definitions" are all very well for most of
the time; but occasionally we find it necessary to take a closer look at them.
I propose now to bring out one or two of my pet hobby-horses and give
them a little exercise: you can crack your whips at them, or try to round
them up and corral them—I shan't mind.

I know that most of us here would agree about the great differences
which exist between the two classifications of artists—the *creative* and the
*interpretative* artist; and for a long time now I have been a member of

159

that small camp—it is a noisy and very exciting camp to dwell in—of those who believe the interpretative artist to be a very small creature in comparison with the creative artist. A good deal of our strong feeling about this matter rises from the irritation caused by that indiscriminate adulation which makes up the atmosphere that the interpretative artist continuously breathes. We are revolted by the many stupidities (the gossip about their private lives, the interest that is based on knowing what they eat, what kinds of friends they have, the colour of their underwear, and such idiocies) which don't do any real good to the interpretative artist and which do positively lead to a gradual blotting out of all artistic values in any discussion of their lives and their work. The building up of these people— generally by that very unnecessary type, "the gossip writer"—is always at the expense of the works of art it should be their privilege—and let me emphasise that word *privilege*—to communicate to an audience. We all know that the question isn't one we can easily dispose of; this matter of the consumers or customers having an interest in how their darlings behave when they are not before the public eye is tied up with some very deep-rooted need that nearly all of us feel. It is the need to project ourselves into the person of the principal performer: it goes back to the days of the first interpretative artists, when the form of all art was a primitive religious ceremonial, and the priest or medicine-man was the direct link with those hidden and mysterious forces we call "gods". Everyone in the crowd then wanted passionately to be the key-man who had direct access (as it seemed to all of them there) to the dark unseen powers who moved the winds and the waves and the sun in the sky.

Now, to get back to this comparison between two classes of artists: I know that this analogy I'm going to propose isn't a very exact one, but I think we'll all understand it. I draw the analogy that, as we can divide artists into two groups, creative and interpretative, so we can classify critics into the same two categories.

The first, or creative critic is the kind whose judgment is based very firmly on a breadth of understanding about *everything* connected with the form of art he criticises; his judgment is not based only on that single occasion he is at the moment reviewing. This breadth of understanding depends not only on his having a wide and deep knowledge of the technical and executive processes of the art. It depends just as much on his awareness of the relationship of that form of art to the whole culture which makes the art possible: and also on his sense of the process of historical development which has led that particular art into the form it shows itself in to-day. You will all easily recall from your wide acquaintance with the great critics of both past and present in your own field, that each of them shows clearly in his work this sense of what I can perhaps briefly define as "the historical continuity of art". It shines out of the work of those whom we would all agree in defining as "great critics": I think, for instance, of such a representative half-dozen as C. E. Montague and Bernard Shaw—in his golden youth—, of Levinson and John Martin in the field of theatre dance, of L. C. Knights, Dr Bowra and Edmund Wilson amongst to-day's literary critics. In their work our interest is seized—and held—by the revelation of their sense of the vastness of each form of art, its multiplicity of facets. The best criticism shows us this awareness of the almost unimaginable magnitude of each of the major forms of art produced out of our civilisation; and also an awareness—parallel with the first one—of our human inability ever to master all the knowledge, theories, reasonings, explanations which exist about each separate one of the great forms of art.

Perhaps the briefest definition of what I've christened the "interpretative" critic is that he is one who can measure off the worth of a particular performance, a novel, a poem, a work of music or painting, judged directly on its first impact—and nothing more. It is, I suppose, a judgment based only, *and always only,* on his direct emotional reaction to the work, but quite unrelated to the vast processes which first brought that form of art into existence. And of course we all bear in mind all the time the fact that the critic, of whatever kind, has to have a more highly developed receptivity to the emotion that a work of art can arouse than the casual consumer of that form of art. This latter kind of criticism is, as we are all too well aware, the kind most commonly found to-day; the danger is, that when it is practised with something less than the completely objective frame of mind, it can—and so often does—degenerate into an assessment of the personality who wrote, or played, or acted, or danced the work which is being judged. The actor becomes much more important than the play, and the playwright sinks into the background—he is merely a name somewhere in an obscure corner of the programme.

We are all aware of the strange changes that occur in the arts through the mere process of the passing of time: music quite literally sounds differently, because the technique of making instruments changes, and newer materials are used, and there are more highly organised methods of building the instruments. Novels produce on their readers an effect other than that which the author intended—because changes have grown into the absolute structure of the society in which those particular novels were written. Differences about moral, social, political and philosophical values have created a very differently balanced attitude of mind on the part of the reader, listener, or dilettante of the arts: he no longer agrees with the author's point-of-view about whether This is Right and That is Wrong. We have all seen actors playing parts not in pursuance of the playwright's intent, but in pursuance of certain aims known only to themselves and their press-agents—but this is a kind of change which I'm sure plays have always been subjected to: think of Nahum Tate rewriting—was it *King Lear?*—to give it a happy ending! Now, unless the critic is aware that these changes do occur—and go on occurring—he is in danger of estimating the work of art on the same mental and emotional level as the—what I must call—"average customer" who has bought the novel or paid for the theatre seat. When he writes all his valuations in those sorts of terms he is in the greatest danger of his whole career—he will tend more and more to value the work of art as only an immediate piece of work happening here and now—in *this* town on *this* day, and he will cease to be able even to see that its whole justification is the four, or five, or thousand, or tens of thousands of years of human struggle which lie behind the formation of that particular kind of artistic expression.

It seems to me that none of the arts is worth that close study and passionate interest which the critic must show, unless it is perceived as a minute part of the whole pattern of all human endeavour. Our most elementary studies in the arts teach us that their forms are changing under the subtle pressures of the gradually changing background which shapes our daily lives. These very obvious changes are ample evidence that the arts matter because they are alive, and they are showing themselves alive by revealing this slow—but absolutely non-stop—process of change.

If I may go back to the other of our basic definitions: whatever differences may come up when, amongst ourselves, we try to define the word "art", we would probably all agree that it is the result of the conflict between the creative artist's vision, and the actual world around him. Goethe put it very pointedly when he said: "Art is called 'Art' simply because it is not Nature". Our knowledge that each one of us is not only the product of his immediate ancestors, but of generation beyond generation before them—together with the knowledge that we have each one of us been influenced since the moment of birth by a hundred personalities, a thousand incidents—this is what gives us a proper sense of the true and fundamental value of the arts. For they are both the greatest mystery in human existence and possibly the greatest justification for existence; they seem to me to be the only key to understanding what our lives are about. They are the unfinished—and perhaps totally unending—process of struggle between Man and the Universe—or maybe I should say, Man and his efforts to understand, make some kind of sense out of the Universe. I expect I'm making it quite clear that this is the attitude of an agnostic.

I continue to feel, and have so felt for a long time, that the longer we hold our interest in any of the arts, the more we grapple with an understanding of it, the more we must be made aware that the creation, sharing, discussing, propaganding works of art is the biggest thing that men have yet indulged in. I believe it could be shown from a study of history that making and participating in works of art has been the one *entirely non-destructive* activity that mankind has so far found. They explain, though only partly, and are in turn explained by, again only partly, the many philosophies, religions, political systems that Man has so far evolved. They are the triumph—purely, of course, a temporary one—of Man over the natural world he has to inhabit.

Now, our understanding of them (such as it is) should lead us to want to protect as well as to encourage the artist; he isn't superhuman, he's only a different kind of human being; he needs not worship but understanding... and we can understand him even when he doesn't understand himself. And isn't it about time that we all admitted what each of us thinks to himself— and really *knows*—about this business of criticism? that it is through us and our like in all the other countries and cultures that the artist's work is made known, evaluated, kept in circulation, elucidated where necessary, recorded in history? The artist of the future has much to learn from us— but only if we have written the history of our times in a fair and objective and painstaking fashion.

I apologise for stating so much that is obvious, but we must agree that if we are aware of the value to humanity of the arts and of artists and also of the finest kind of criticism—what I have called "creative criticism"—then we must show and maintain some of that proper pride in our function which, deep down, we all feel. That pride is the outward show of the integrity without which none of us dare call his soul his own: and the integrity must be there to balance that humility in the face of the arts which we, next to the creative artists, are so strongly aware of. We feel this smallness of our essential selves as compared with the vast, partly-mysterious, process of art much more keenly than those people—however they are interested in art—who are farther away from the business of making and spreading it.

That humility is a very real thing for us; it grows out of our knowledge of the depth, the size, the wonderful complexity of every one of the arts—all of them alive, full of meaning and intense value; and they *are* alive—real, strong, moving forces—because their value is tied up with that inexplicable something that enables us, even drives us, to go on living... If I've leaned hard on certain things which are very obvious to each one of us I apologise; but I wanted to make clear how important I think it is that we're aware of this difference between "creative" and "interpretative" critics. It's extra-ordinary how many people there are who haven't the smallest idea what it means to be a critic of the arts: it's really quite hard to get some people to realise that you don't "just sit down in front of a typewriter and say whether you liked it or not"—that was how someone put it to me only recently. There is an attitude that places the critic as a kind of peculiar and harmless "backroom boy" in a newspaper office—somebody without the qualifications to be "a real reporter". A great deal of this is due to a kind of transposed enmity on the part of a lot of people who, sensing that we are the ones who most disapprove of the extreme adulation of the inter-pretative artist, get a form of revenge out of assessing us as beings of no real importance to the arts.

Now I want to refer again to this matter of the critic having a sense of the "historical development of art". It seems to me at least as important today as it ever was in the earlier periods of intensive study and propaganding of the arts; this present-day importance hangs on one fact—a fact we are all aware of, I suggest, only partly consciously—and that is the impact of modern changes in our way of life as they react upon, and are in turn influenced by the arts.

Think back on the changes that have come into the way of life of nearly all civilised mankind since the beginning of this century. The increased speed of communication, for one thing, has completely annihilated distance; the new industrial and manufacturing and distributive processes that are a consequence of electrical and chemical advances—all these have had for three or four decades, and are still having, a weighty influence on the general pattern of life for millions of people. We have had the greatest single social change—I mean a compelled alteration in the entire shape and conditioning of a whole society, in Russia—inside this half-century; as well as two of the most brutal and destructive wars men have ever engaged in . . . Now all these changes in how we eat, what we wear, the news we gather from all mankind, these things affect what we feel and think about all the components of our pattern of life; they affect what we feel about the arts, what we get out of, as well as what we put into, the arts. Briefly we have acquired a higher *tempo* and a more intense complexity to the shape of living inside Western civilisation and I suggest that those factors cannot help influencing not only what reward art gives us, they also influence what each of the members of our civilisation puts into the arts—whether he is the creator, performer, distributor, critic or consumer of art.

When any form of art suddenly hits the consciousness of a new layer of public which hadn't, up to that point, been very interested in it, there

comes immediately a process of simplifying, weakening, cheapening it—fc
the new "mass consumption". This means the making of vast amounts c
"Kitsch" in that art-form. In the particular field which most interests m(
(ballet) I see this process occurring now; a great deal of deliberately fifth-
rate ballet is being quite openly created for consumption by a public avid
for a new kind of theatre fare . . . Now how far is it the critic's business to
study these developments—to have a firm viewpoint—and to use all his
energies to counteract these vulgarising processes?

I contend that it is very much our responsibility to fight against all these
vulgarisations; we have to stand by certain first principles, keep on
preaching on behalf of basic principles about each art-form; it is not and
never will be anyone else's job but the critic's, to protect the arts from all
this vulgarity and playing down to mass appetites—appetites which
anyhow cannot be satisfied until the people concerned have acquired some
kind of idea of the value of the form of art they have been led into lusting
for—all of a sudden.

I have dealt in detail with certain very simple and obvious matters to do
with the critic's trade; because although I am sure that we all know how
much valuable work we can perform, we must also realise that very few
people outside such a group as this recognise the particular importance of
our function.

All of us, I am sure, put the ultimate seal of our approval and total
admiration on the artist who shows that very rare quality—humility. We
ourselves know in our hearts that it is a quality that we must show in
connection with our work for the arts. But today that humility has to be
matched with a certain amount of arrogance—in order to get ourselves
accepted at a proper valuation. ... It is, I am sure, unnecessary to mention
that our greatest asset is our acceptance of the idea that there should
always be a state of "cold war" between artists and critics; for private
friendships can undermine the very qualities which make our criticism a
worthwhile activity for each one of us. We don't need to try to pick the
artists' brains to find what they are working towards—we can get all that
we need to know from studying their works; as I said before, it is our
business to understand them even when they don't understand themselves.

*Index*

# Index

169

*Index*                                                                173

Lightning Source UK Ltd.
Milton Keynes UK
20 March 2010

151636UK00001B/44/P